SCIENCE EDUCATION:
A Minds-On Approach
for the Elementary Years

SCIENCE EDUCATION:
A Minds-On Approach
for the Elementary Years

Eleanor Duckworth
Harvard University

Jack Easley
University of Illinois at Urbana-Champaign

David Hawkins
University of Colorado

Androula Henriques
University of Geneva

with an Introduction
by Deborah J. Trumbull
Cornell University

LEA LAWRENCE ERLBAUM ASSOCIATES, PUBLISHERS
1990 Hillsdale, New Jersey   Hove and London

Lawrence Erlbaum Associates, Inc., Publishers
365 Broadway
Hillsdale, New Jersey 07642

Library of Congress Cataloging-in-Publication Data

Science Education

Includes indexes.
1. Science—Study and teaching (Elementary)
I. Duckworth, Eleanor Ruth.
LB1585.E396   1990
372.3'5044   88-36331

Printed in United States of America
10   9   8   7   6   5   4   3   2

Contents

Preface

The necessity of teaching science in elementary school is no longer questioned. Nowadays, everyone is convinced that children have the right to be properly introduced to science as they are to mathematics, language, music, or painting. This is not only because it might facilitate further scientific studies for them in the future, but because, while they are children, it is enriching for them to understand more about so-called physical phenomena and to sense the excitement of the researcher when he or she examines the mysteries of the world. Within the limits of their capacity, children have the right to understand the human activity called *science*.

In spite of this consensus about science teaching in elementary school, it is still not a common practice, mainly because it is very difficult enterprise. Many essential problems have not been clarified and many important questions remain to be answered. For example:

- Are children ages 7 to 12 able to use a scientific method to gather and verify information?
- How do they "read" an experiment?
- What questions and problems seem interesting to them?
- What sort of teacher training is required? Is it possible for someone without a scientific background to become a good science teacher, and how?
- If it is impossible to teach young children "our" science, the

science of the late 20th century, can we, teachers, allow children to create "their" science, as scientists of Antiquity and of the Middle Ages created theirs?

As a matter of fact, when children become pupils they already know a lot about many many things: letters, numbers, physical phenomena, adult behavior, and so on. When they first go to a science class, they have already begun to elaborate some kind of theory on the topic taught—and this theory often differs from child to child. How do these ideas interfere with the teaching? To what extent must a teacher take them into account?

The question that follows from this is: If children, as thinking beings, elaborate theories independently of systematic teaching, what do they make of that systematic teaching? Do they treat it as an isolated unit or do they try to articulate it with their own ideas?

A question of a somewhat different nature, but not less important than the others, is the following: What kind of relation must the science lessons have with the other disciplines? Particularly with mathematics? Furthermore, if in the last analysis, science teaching requires a really active method, can it be inserted just like that in a traditional school?

In this volume, four authors from different professional backgrounds, but who have all devoted an important part of their lives to the problems of science teaching in the elementary school, present their reflections on this subject. The complementary nature of our views is seen in the analysis of the role played by the four principal factors of the game called "science teaching," namely the teacher, the child, the topics, and the methods—which is the focal point of this volume. We hope that it will help teachers who wish to let their pupils taste something of the human activity that we call *science*.

Androula Henriques

1

Introduction

Deborah J. Trumbull
Cornell University

The poet Seamus Heaney said that landscape is sacramental, to be read as text. Earth is instinct: perfect, irrational, semiotic. If I read winter right, it is a scroll—the white growing wider and wider like the sweep of an arm—and from it we gain a peripheral vision, a capacity for what Nabokov calls "those asides of spirit, those footnotes in the volume of life by which we know life and find it to be good."

—Gretel Ehrlich (1985)

On a recent visit to retired relatives in Arizona, we planned a trip to the Grand Canyon for a visitor who had never been there. Winter snows eliminated the chance for hiking, but we felt that visits to several of the roadside viewpoints would allow an introduction to the world of the Canyon.

Community opinion leaders insisted we stop at The Movie, which they described as wonderful and fantastic. The movie screen was several stories high and all the latest technology had been used for making The Movie. I was not enthusiastic about spending 30 minutes watching a movie depicting the reality we would soon see, but thought that perhaps The Movie would, by increasing my understanding, inform my vision and help me to see the Canyon better. I speculated that The Movie would explain some of the assorted bits of information I tried to study before each visit—names and ages of the various rock types and strata, the various geologic events that created the Canyon, the present ecology—in some way that would enable me to remember them for more than an afternoon.

As we embarked on the 2-hour trip we were a bit concerned that we would not find The Movie. However, as we turned on to the road leading to the park entrance we were met by a billboard announcing "The number one tourist attraction," The Movie. I wondered how the billboard designers would characterize the Grand Canyon itself. We bought tickets and filed into the theater, making our way to seats the opinion leaders had assured us would allow the fullest appreciation of The Movie.

The theater itself was an experience, even before The Movie began. The sharply raked seats and huge screen were disconcerting and disturbing. The scale was all wrong. The huge screen dominated the room, dwarfing everything else. The floor was angled so steeply that each row of seats seemed isolated, unprotected by a row in front. I felt in imminent danger of loosing my balance and tumbling down to land in a heap at the foot of the screen. My vertigo was not relieved when the film began, for what minimal narrative there was was regularly interspersed with footage shot from planes speeding over the canyon rim or skimming the surface of the river in the bottom of the Grand Canyon. The slight plot structure concerned primarily the exploits and experiences of Europeans who had explored the Canyon. There were a few dramatic shots of Canyon fauna or flora—the arachnophobes in the audience gasped at the image of a spider enlarged to the size of a three-story building. But there was nothing about the geology, ecology, or history of the Canyon.

I left The Movie feeling overwhelmed and disoriented, not enlightened. I had vicariously experienced swooping down the Canyon in some kind of flying machine and learned what the raging waters of the Colorado River looked like close up. I had nearly made myself seasick by trying to watch shadows, filmed from a moving camera, progress across the Canyon rim. The Movie gave me no further understanding of the Canyon nor of what it would be like to visit the Canyon as a human being, propelled by my own efforts. There was nothing to serve as a guide, an invitation, or an impetus to further encounters.

Why spend so much time describing some vexatious tourist trap? "Relax," I can hear a reader say, "it was only a 30-minute movie, for heaven's sake. Don't make such a big deal out of it." The analogy may be stretched, but The Movie seemed like much of what one reads about education. A researcher or theoretician swoops down on a group of students or classrooms or schools, records a few isolated features of the landscape, does an experiment or illustrates a point, makes a few more records, then leaves and later publishes The Report. Readers of The

Report are as passive as viewers of The Movie, presented with someone else's interpretation of features these others considered important. In most reports readers see *only* those things deemed important or thrilling by the writer and can learn very little of the other features of the setting, its history, political and social context, and the people involved. Readers are generally able to envision neither how they might have acted in the particular situation nor what they might do to remedy the difficulty identified or repeat the success reported. As with viewing The Movie, readers of The Report have, at best, a pseudoexperience. The effect is numbing and stultifying rather than enlightening and invigorating.

The authors of this volume are not of the "swoop-and-report" school of educational study. The chapters in this book are richly detailed reports from people who have explored elementary science education in depth, in many settings, and for extended periods of time. The chapters tell of ongoing work and, often, how the work and the people have changed over time.

The stories told by these authors are important to consider now. Once again elementary science education has come around on the carousel of reform issues. We in education are, again, implored or commanded to improve the quality of American school children's knowledge of science and of mathematics to enable them to become good citizens, good engineers, or good researchers.

Many new reform efforts are similar to ones proposed earlier, suggesting little learning from history. However, the authors of these chapters have been seriously involved with efforts for change that began within earlier reform projects, and they have learned from that previous work. They have continued to work, and reflect, and work some more on difficult issues in elementary science education. The concerns and views expressed in these different chapters are generally complementary, although they address elementary science education from different vantage points. They describe work with many of the same raw materials—water, shadows, images—and offer various views about the use of such materials and the related topics. Sometimes their views are conflicting. The ideas raised in these chapters can richly reverberate with each other and with ideas in the minds of readers, contributing to an increased vision, understanding, and commitment to action.

One feature that characterizes all the authors is their strong faith that human beings love to learn and that all of us are driven by a fine curiosity to make sense and order of the puzzlement of our worlds. A concern these authors share is that schooling, as commonly structured, may extinguish any natural driving curiosity. This curtailment does not have to occur, and these chapters present numerous rich examples of projects that have worked. They tell about students of different ages, backgrounds, and abilities who have been involved in authentic struggles to learn about the science in their worlds. Through reading about the experiences of these authors we learn also about their thinking and about what it has meant to be committed to the kind of work they do. These chapters are filled with vital traces of people who care, struggle, make mistakes, learn and grow.

The chapters of this book can be read in any order. The purpose of this introductory chapter is to provide some framework for readers. There are any number of ways to do this, but I propose to do so in a way influenced by my experiences as a science teacher and teacher educator. After several readings of these chapters, it made most sense to me to select some of the areas that I found most illuminated, often from quite different perspectives, by these authors. Some of these areas are ones I have explored in my work and others involve deep-seated assumptions held by the authors that are less completely explicated in these writings. I hope that this approach will continue and extend the dialogue between these chapters and other readers.

After commenting about the nature of this book—for it seems a rare creature—it makes sense to discuss the critique of schooling implicit in these chapters. The critique is driven by the writers' conceptualizations of science, learning, curriculum, and the preferred roles for teachers and students. I discuss each of these interrelated conceptions. After this discussion I describe some of the changes the writers suggest and the implications of these changes for teacher education and education generally.

THE NATURE OF THE BOOK

The intent of this book is to reformulate elementary science teaching. Many proposals for reform, whether prepared by one author or several, have a standard format. Current failings are documented, blame is parcelled out to various groups, a theory rationalizing the reform is presented, and the proposed new curriculum is described in careful technical detail. Generally much care is given to describing precisely the new curriculum. Much less care is given to descriptions of how the new curriculum is enacted in classrooms, the ways teachers and students can be engaged.

These authors do not follow this standard plan. The book presents no curricula with delineated learning objectives, goals, assessment instruments, feedback loops, or other impedimenta of rationalized planning.

It does, however, describe teachers and students at work doing science. These descriptions present a kind of curriculum document. Duckworth, for example, suggests that a curriculum should be considered as a vehicle to involve students in thinking about matters that are considered to be important. The stories told by these authors engage the reader in thinking about matters central to elementary science teaching. And, as we readers learn what children and teachers worked well on, we gain insight into important activities that can occur in classrooms. The vivid accounts and detailed analyses provided in these chapters suggest to us new ways of being teachers and students: ways that have worked. We can begin to understand some of our failures and can see some new ways of being and acting as teachers and as students. There will be readers who have worked out some of these problems, so can gain support for their work. The changes needed to implement this "curriculum" do not simply involve using new worksheets or texts. These changes require substantial shifts in how we think of our work as teachers and as learners. Make no mistake, the changes proposed in this book are *fundamental* changes.

Just as they can be considered curriculum documents, these chapters can be considered research reports although they contain few of the trappings typically associated with "educational research." There are no pre- and postmeasures, no tables presenting results of complicated statistical analyses, no detailed discussion of sampling techniques. Rather, there are descriptions of actual work done, descriptions similar to those of naturalists encountering new habitats. The nature of these chapters reflects the authors' conception of how science is actually done. The work described by these authors starts from a theoretical stance, generally one strongly influenced by Piaget. The authors have then developed some approach to teaching based in the theory, carried out and evaluated that teaching. The "results" and "evidence" presented to us allow us to share somewhat in the experiments and the construction of a theory or approach.

THE CRITIQUE OF SCHOOLING

A central assumption shared by these authors is that, too often, existing school structures in elementary education deny autonomy to the actors in those settings. Most approaches to instruction assume that children should be passive learners or, if active, should have freedom to act only to meet the goals set by others. As a result, pupils do not learn how to direct their own learning activities or to set their own goals for learning. Little authentic thinking and questioning go on; in fact, these are discouraged, particularly when teachers feel unsure of their own knowledge.

The hierarchical governance structures operating in many school systems and the specialized roles given to school personnel serve to limit the autonomy of teachers. Too frequently teachers are treated as technicians, mere implementors of others' plans. Outside experts identify the appropriate content and sequencing of science topics. Commercial textbooks, curriculum guides, and prepared materials require teachers to carry out procedures developed by others. Efforts to provide accountability, directed by national, state, and local governing bodies responding to perceived public demand, hold teachers responsible for ensuring that their students can demonstrate knowledge by performing well on standardized tests.

When children are taught within this context, they may learn to do well on standardized tests but may also learn that school content is produced by experts who have discovered the truth. If some of the "truths" studied in school science do not make sense to them, children resort to memorization. Such experiences can easily lead students to assume that they cannot learn or make sense of the science subject matter. They can doubt their ability to think and reason about science. They are thus rendered unable to challenge authoritarian or dogmatic statements ascribed to scientists, or even to think that such statements can be open to challenge.

Much subject matter, including elementary science, is taught as an accumulation of facts or generalizations that are unconnected to the everyday lives and interests of students. As the authors of these chapters illustrate, everyday experiences may seem to lie outside or to contradict the generalizations taught in school science lessons. Most teachers are unable or unwilling to probe these apparent contradictions when students point them out. Rather, contradictions are ignored or inadequately explained away. The student pointing out a contradiction is characterized as stupid, obstreperous, or one prone to challenge authority. Children are discouraged from thinking they can use science knowledge in their own lives.

Learning in schools is primarily considered to be an individual process. Children are repeatedly admonished to "do your own work." This emphasis on individual effort too easily turns learning into a competitive endeavor. Cooperation among students on their work is usually considered cheating. The stricture against working together ignores the social aspects of coming to know. The benefits of learning how to argue one's beliefs based on evidence and change beliefs based on companions' work are not realized.

Schools further contribute to the isolation of individuals by compartmentalizing subject matter. An authentic science project may spill naturally into a writing project, an art project, a mathematics project. The unnatural separation of subject matters begins early and contributes to older students' well-documented inabilities to use "math skills" in biology exercises or biology knowledge in working problems in chemistry.

These are not new condemnations of schooling. They have been made by researchers who explicate the hidden curriculum of schools, examine the roles that schools play in perpetuating societal inequities, and the curriculum theorists who address the ways in which technocratic curriculum structures reify and objectify knowledge. For example, Willis (1978) documented in heartbreaking detail how high school pupils' refusal to submit to the control of schooling results in patterns that, rather than resisting the schools' power to perpetuate social inequities, contributes to their continuance. Strains of these critiques are less commonly heard from science and mathematics educators. These are important critiques for they help us to explain certain kinds of school failures and to delineate the pressures that resist reform.

The approaches to the teaching of elementary science advocated by these authors assume much of this critique and present us with viable alternatives. The stories told by these authors show us that negative effects of schooling are not inevitable. Change can occur. Given the right conditions, students can act autonomously and responsibly control their own learning projects. Teachers will need to develop new ways to structure classrooms and work assignments. New social rules and arrangements in classrooms can allow students to work together to learn science and do science in elementary classrooms. Teachers and pupils alike have to change their ways of thinking about what it means to learn science in schools.

Many of the changes suggested are complementary to changes urged by the writing-as-process movement, which also stresses authentic learning (see, e.g., Mayher, Lester, & Pradl, 1983; Miller 1987; Moffett, 1968, 1985). The approach aims to help students use writing to express their ideas. When students begin such a writing program, they are even free to invent their own spellings and grammar as they rush to express their thoughts on paper. As students progress in the writing-as-process they are encouraged to help each other, to critique each other's work, and to respect each other as serious writers. Much work concerned with teaching reading comprehension also stresses student autonomy and sense making. Clearly, there are many people working with similar aims. This book then is also timely because complementary approaches to learning in other subject areas in elementary education are flourishing.

SCIENCE

These authors endeavor to portray science as it is actually practiced and not as it has been portrayed by the logical positivists and their descendants. The authors stress the playfulness of science, an emphasis that should bring joy to lovers of children and childhood. Scientists, as Easley and Hawkins characterize them, play with ideas in their attempts to reduce the complexities they study to simple and elegant summaries or generalizations. Crucial to any scientific work is a thoroughgoing exploration of and familiarity with the phenomenon studied. The playfulness of the scientist, like the playfulness of a child, is intense, but permits the freedom to explore and try out a wide range of ideas with no fear of being wrong. Eventually an idea or an analogy will allow the scientist to make sense of observed events and to develop a coherent explanation.

The next facet of doing science entails developing an explicit argument sufficient to convince others that the analogy or idea does make sense of the complexities studied. Because others must also be persuaded, science as it is practiced is a social activity. Individual insights or discoveries are of no importance unless the relevant science community can be convinced of their salience. Further, science is not just a social, but an argumentative activity. Evidence must be carefully collected and arrayed to develop a compelling case; thus the need for thorough and systematic exploration of phenomena. In scientific areas undergoing intense investigation, disagreement is the norm. Agreement among scientists is a creation of textbook writers and does not reflect the activity of scientists. Scientists work with no hope of finding final answers. The scientific enterprise entails the prospect of being surprised, of getting new results that challenge one's previous notions.

The hope that these authors share is that elementary classrooms can allow intense exploration, argument construction, and dialogue among pupils similar to that which occurs as scientists go about doing science. It is difficult work to organize a classroom in which these activities can occur. Some of the authors explicitly address teacher actions and expectations that are needed to foster such a classroom. The role of the teacher is addressed in more detail later.

These authors imply that all scientific research is grounded in understandings developed through extended exploration of the phenomenon being investigated. Sometimes these understandings will be the result of systematic investigation, sometimes they will develop tacitly, with no conscious effort or awareness. No scientist begins a project by abandoning preexisting knowledge. Rather, new work starts with what the researcher already understands. Hawkins refers to this preexisting and often unarticulated knowledge as common sense and holds that it forms the basis for the development and investigation of all new questions. Obviously, what is common sense for elementary pupils will not be common sense for a grizzled biologist, but the processes of knowledge construction will be analogous.

All students, of any age, have common sense knowledge about the world. A first step in learning more about natural phenomena is to trigger the curiosity that will impel students to examine their common sense understandings. Duckworth describes this as "opening up the world" and develops seemingly simple exercises that enable students to examine systematically phenomena that were so taken for granted as to be unproblematic, virtually invisible. Once noticed, everyday phenomena can be examined through activities that are analogous to the work of "real" scientists. The work described by these authors makes clear that everyday phenomena can be intensively and fruitfully investigated by students of all ages. The results of these intensive investigations may, or may not, correspond to accepted science views.

Some proponents of discovery learning assume that, if the teacher organizes and directs work carefully enough, students will come to the same principles or generalizations of science texts. These authors do not make that assumption. The aim is for students to explore earnestly and to think carefully so explanations and hypotheses can be tested by further work with the phenomenon. These authors actually vary in the degree to which they think it essential that students articulate a coherent explanation or reach a consensus among themselves. All agree, however, that students will have a much clearer idea of how to investigate the phenomenon and of why the questions asked by scientists about that phenomenon are important.

Another advantage of studying ordinary phenomena with ordinary materials is that, as Duckworth points out, many fascinating ordinary events are not well explained by textbooks. Students, therefore, must develop their own model or explanation because they cannot find one in a text to see if they agree. They must learn to support their own work by thinking through their own explanations and experiments and using their own vocabularies. In the process they begin to communicate clearly without resorting to vocabularies memorized in former lessons or culled unthinkingly from texts. And, they learn to evaluate their own work.

The power of students taking on their own investigations is hard to overestimate. These authors offer many examples of the benefits.

LEARNING

As viewed by these authors, learning is not an efficient process that can be planned, structured, organized, and streamlined. Certain conditions can facilitate children's learning and other conditions can render learning almost impossible. But within these limits, the progress of learning can be quite unpredictable. Knowledge about a science topic is not something that can be broken into parts, packaged, and transmitted to students in digestible bits. Students must work and make sense of material through extended exploration, experimentation, and discussion. We can and must try to establish optimal conditions in which the process takes place, but we must never be surprised or disappointed if a student follows an unexpected pathway when investigating some phenomenon.

These authors emphasize the importance of students' work with concrete materials. These references are not synonymous with an activity-based approach to science teaching in which children's manipulation of materials is the object. Henriques expresses this distinction most clearly when she states:

> I therefore wish to point out that when we talk of "activity" in the Piagetian sense, we refer to mental activity that cannot be observed as such but that can be inferred from observable indices furnished by the subject (manipulation, verbal explanations, etc.). . . .
>
> Limiting the activity of the subject to the manipulations performed would mean that one considers the object as the main factor in the construction of knowledge. If the object were the main factor, we would be at a loss to explain why the same objects manipulated yield such different results in terms of the knowledge acquired. (p. 143)

Henriques also clearly expresses a point regarding students' existing notions about the science topic studied, a point implied by other authors in this book. Recently, research to elicit children's existing notions about science topics (referred to variously as misconceptions, alternative conceptions, or children's science) has prospered. Teachers and teacher educators can respond to the findings of this research in different ways. One response has been to argue that students' existing notions are so idiosyncratic and confused that the only sensible thing to do is to ignore them, and to teach the scientifically accepted notions carefully and well. Another response to the existence of student preconceptions has been to enjoin teachers to develop methods designed to elicit students' existing notions. Teachers then work to change wrong ideas by presenting contradictory evidence.

Henriques' response to student misconceptions is informed by the Piagetian belief that learners will assimilate new things according to their existing notions. The assimilation process renders it very difficult to know what the right conflicting data will be because, through assimilation, students may not perceive any conflict. Henriques' response is that teachers should provide chances for students to express their views throughout instruction, knowing that there will always be "distortions" or misconceptions. What is most important is the process of articulating and thinking about children's conceptions rather than the elimination of "wrong" ones. Henriques' work demonstrates that even young students can argue and construct experiments to test their conceptions.

CURRICULUM

Curriculum is conceptualized by these authors in a fashion that differs radically from the rationalistic and technocratic view so common in schools today. The common view of curriculum assumes that learning can be made efficient and stresses carefully structured prepared materials with clearly stated learning goals and specific objectives. Objective tests are designed to measure the achievement of the prespecified goals and objectives. There are many factors that make the common view of curriculum attractive. One factor, which relates directly to the concerns of this book, is the nature of classroom life. Many writers have elucidated the complexity of classrooms—there are always more things to do than can be done, more changes happening than one teacher can keep track of, more needs to be met than can be—and all this occurs in a volatile milieu. The number of decisions a teacher must make in one day is staggering.

Teachers and other school personnel will understandably seize on those arrangements that can reduce complexity and uncertainty. One way to do so is to clarify tasks in the classroom. If learning is divided into discrete tasks, in neat units with objective exams, the teacher can gain a feeling of control and order. He or she can also gain a feeling of accomplishment. The teacher can aver that the students have covered this material and passed these quizzes, and so the teacher can be secure that he or she can move on to the next unit. By keeping a record of things accomplished, the teacher can achieve a sense of having done something, met some goals, delivered some intellectual content, instilled some skills. A school administrator can assure him or herself that the students are making progress and that the teachers are producing results. Parents can have evidence that their youngsters are progressing in their march toward knowledge.

Pressures for accountability are often based on and contribute to the technical view of curriculum. Demands that students pass tests developed by external experts push teachers to cover material likely to be on the tests. These tests may be poorly structured so that a significant share of success is a function of skill at taking tests. In fact, teachers may coach students on how to take tests. These tests also often focus on easily measured, simple aspects of the subject. State or district mandated curricula, often the basis for paper-and-pencil multiple choice tests, reinforce the technocratic view of curriculum.

The kind of science curriculum espoused in this volume is not one that provides a carefully delineated pathway to a predetermined, clear-cut, and easily measured terminus. The authors share a view of learning as a messy and unpredictable process. These writers all agree, I believe, that the way to communicate about curriculum is to share stories about projects initiated by students in classrooms, illustrating what happened as pupils were engaged in making meaning of materials. Some of these writers seem to think that pupils, with some assistance, will move toward understandings that represent the scientifically accepted views. Others focus more on the processes students use to make sense of the material and are less concerned that they move toward accepted views.

Curriculum conceived of as stories told by careful observers will allow readers to learn about projects that interested students of different kinds and in different settings. The science curriculum espoused by these authors requires that students work with materials that interest them and that allow for and yield to exploration. Sophisticated and complex science teaching materials that cannot be extensively modified are not needed and will, in fact, usually be a detriment to learning. Curriculum stories can describe the materials that led to sustained questioning and interaction and the aspects of things students seized on and wished to explore. Readers of these stories can learn ways to get their own students involved in projects by gaining an idea of what other pupils found interesting.

As these writers all indicate, when students have the freedom to explore a science project their investigations may lead them in many different directions. There will really be no endpoints to science learning because the more that students have explored and learned about a phenomenon, the more there will be to learn about it. Such a stance can be exciting and liberating. It can also strike terror into the hearts of teachers who worry about the unknown. Curriculum as stories about what has happened in other times and places can prepare teachers and provide them with some idea of what things are likely to happen when their students work on a particular science project. Curriculum stories can also show teachers the benefits and problems that might accompany particular projects.

TEACHERS' ROLES

Many teachers have fears about teaching science because, since they are not experts, they feel they will give students wrong information. However, these writers argue that teachers do not have to be experts. Science, as done now, is so specialized that the expertise of any accomplished scientist is quite limited. It is impossible to be a science expert in more than a few areas. Once out of their specialization, most scientists themselves work with everyday notions that would not be acceptable to experts in that field. If scientists cannot be general experts, teachers and teacher educators should not expect to be experts in the subject matter.

The previous points on the role of common sense knowledge in scientific research should also allay some fears. As Hawkins makes clear in his recognition of the role of common sense knowledge gleaned from acting in the world, the abstract generalizations of a mature scientist may have little use in the practical daily problems one confronts. Aristotelian physics works well in daily life. It is really no problem if students generate some now scientifically outmoded explanations of force and acceleration. Their explorations will prepare them for later advanced study of these same topics.

Good teachers, acting from concern and a sense of duty, often assume they must be responsible for the learning that goes on in their classes. This responsibility requires that teachers guide and monitor the pupils' learning, picking them up when they stumble, providing them with the right answers when they question, providing the right questions to help them practice the correct answers. This role places great demands on teachers. If they feel ill-prepared in the subject matter, this role becomes even more difficult. Good teachers who feel they have had insufficient background in science may avoid science teaching, use "science" as a time to let students work on fun activities, or become quite authoritarian in their teaching of science, focusing on unquestioning memorization. None of these responses helps students learn any topic deeply or learn about the doing of science.

These authors expect a different role for teachers. They agree that teachers will best facilitate student science learning by selecting engaging materials, arousing student curiosity about these materials and creating a supportive climate in which students can work. What else is necessary? There are differences among the views of these authors. These differences are subtle, sometimes tacit, and interesting. The differences seem, to me, to center around the amount of current accepted scientific knowledge the teacher needs and the degree to which the teacher must direct the activities of children.

Do teachers need to know enough of the particular topic to be able to encourage those student activities that relate most directly to current scientific notions? Do teachers need to know the developing literature on children's common misconceptions so that they can design on-the-spot exercises that will challenge these misconceptions? Is it enough for students to discuss and argue topics extensively, or should they also be accountable for articulating their conclusions in some formal fashion? What should teachers do, other than maintain order, while students are working on science projects? How do teachers know work on science projects is going well? These are all questions answered somewhat differently by these authors.

Henriques addresses some of these very directly. She states that teachers do not really need to answer student questions, for students are quite able and willing to construct answers. She does indicate that teachers learn to help students work by asking questions that extend student thinking. Good questions will not ask for "right answers" (i.e., use of correct vocabulary or recall of memorized but meaningless words). Rather, good questions help the child to think further and more explicitly. Teachers will need to learn how to ask sincere questions, not the kind that imply some expected right answer. From this, students can learn that adults are interested in and value their thinking. This respect should give students the confidence to develop their own thinking. The proper response to students questions is often a dilemma for teachers.

Many concerned teachers have told me that their students expect them, as teachers, to know all the answers. Those teachers with the necessary confidence make a concerted effort to disabuse students of this expectation of omniscience. However, the response these secure teachers often give to students is, "I don't know, but let's go look it up," rather than, "I don't know. What do you think? What do you already know? How would you figure it out?" These well-meaning teachers, then, may perpetuate the myth of the authoritative science text and disregard the students own abilities to construct meanings.

A respect for students' efforts to make sense of a topic does not mean that teachers have less of a role to play. Teachers cannot be responsible for students' learning, as though it were a deliverable product, but they can and must monitor the processes students are using as they work. Henriques provides a system for characterizing the ways in which students can be involved in activities. Each type of involvement has an important role in learning, so students should experience them all.

It is possible to interpret a plea for increased student autonomy as reducing the responsibility teachers have. This is not the case. The role of teacher held by these authors requires much skill and effort. The teacher needs to identify projects that will interest students, monitor their work by asking questions that will further the work, help them learn how to work together.

STUDENT ROLES

We need to allow students to be the children they are, to allow them to play and explore phenomena of interest. We need to avoid or reduce a fear of being "wrong," and encourage their delight at the unexpected. Children's curiosity, whetted by the clever teacher, needs to become the impetus for much of their work on science projects. If conditions are right, students will also learn to choose their own goals, direct their own work, and evaluate their own explanations.

These expectations often conflict with the lives children are leading in America. Schooling in America—not day care, but schooling—is being extended to younger and younger children. It is not enough that they make mudpies in the park; now they must take kiddy ecology courses and nature study. There is an increase in the pressure on children, causing them to worry more about right and wrong answers. On the news recently a reporter asked a child of about 10 to define love. The child said "I can't. We haven't studied that in school yet."

PROPOSED CHANGES AND IMPLICATIONS
FOR TEACHER EDUCATION

These chapters call for significant changes in the way elementary science is taught to teachers and to students. In fact, the authors would probably not countenance the preceding phrase, preferring: changes in the way elementary teachers and students learn science and learn about doing science.

The elementary science education envisioned by these authors requires that teachers develop new ways of being and acting as science teachers in their classrooms. Teachers need to gain a better understanding of the processes of doing science so that they realize that science does not discover truth and that the agreed-upon science knowledge is ever changing as a result of continuing argument and counter argument. If teachers could see science in this way, they would be much more able to help students to make their own discoveries in a reasoned, systematic, and public way without worrying as much about wrong conclusions. If they understood the ways in which scientists make meaning, teachers should be able to eschew an authoritarian role and an unquestioning attitude toward the discoveries of science.

Duckworth describes classroom activities she has experienced that allow the development of a changed attitude about science. Her work demonstrates how teachers' experiences as learners in one such classroom can enable them to orchestrate similar classrooms for their teaching.

Hawkins argues that teachers as neophyte science learners probably do need to understand a bit more about science so they can see where activities can lead when their students are working with good science materials. An increased understanding of science will help teachers to develop some sense of productive questions that their pupils can pursue. It seems that Hawkins, and perhaps others, assumes that some questions and explorations are better than others. If this is the case, elementary teachers may need to study more science *in the kind of situation* described by Hawkins.

These authors are describing reform efforts and programs that require intense human effort engaging all of us as teachers and learners. These reform efforts do not involve national, or international, boards of experts designing detailed decrees to be carried out by thousands of teachers and tens of thousands of students. The reform efforts envisioned by these authors require knots of people working together on projects and learning, always, how to work better together and how to find projects that foster this work. Reform efforts are needed in all aspects of the schooling enterprise. These knots of people might be composed of one or two elementary teachers and their pupils, or one or two teacher educators and their preservice teacher pupils, or teacher educators and experienced teachers exploring some science topics together, or preservice teachers working with a small group of elementary pupils on a science topic, or perhaps even a school principal working with one or two elementary teachers and a few pupils to investigate some science topic. There are many locales in the enterprise of schooling where groups of people need to work together to produce real change in elementary science teaching. Work in any of these locales has many implications. Let us explore some.

The vision of science teaching expressed in these chapters requires that those in positions of authority give up the traditional power and control their assumed knowledge has allowed them to exercise. The understanding of the nature of science and knowledge presented in these chapters should aid in the surrender of traditional control. Change will be slow and difficult because students and teachers have had these traditional notions of control inculcated over many years and in many contexts.

As they begin school, youngsters should have fewer inculcated notions about control. As innocents, they will have the easiest time with the kind of science teaching presented in this volume. If this is indeed the case, one of the most fruitful means of abetting the change process would involve inservice and preservice teachers in work with young children. Easley and Henriques, in particular, tell stories that show just how much young children can do. Through genuine work with children, we can learn much about new ways of being teachers.

As we all work to be the kind of teacher that enables our students to develop and to test their own understanding, we must see that our students learn to work with each other and to make public their understandings and puzzlings. To accomplish this purpose, it will be necessary to foster the growth of new patterns of communication and discourse in classrooms. Older students will need to rediscover their voices that became stilled by traditional school practices. And, as these voices develop, fellow students and teachers will need to learn to listen to each other attentively, critically, and with respect. The subtle mechanisms that give increasing power and credibility to the bright, the vocal, and the quick need to be surfaced and dismantled.

Learning new patterns of discourse is not easy. For example, in my graduate seminars I try to encourage student discussion and debate but also want to ensure that they consider their points from the new or different perspectives presented in class readings. I want them to talk, but I also want them to use the concepts and perspectives we are reading to frame that talk. I hope to have the students themselves take more responsibility for directing discussion, but worry how to do so. These are not easy changes. Students are not used to challenging directly each other's interpretations. Students are not used to defending their views in a benevolent environment. I am not used to challenging student views in front of others. These changes may be slowed by my deep belief that, were I to give students explicit directions about how I wanted discussion to develop, these good students would mechanically mimic the behaviors I describe but not the intents. We all leave many class sessions frustrated. But slowly, the discussions begun in class continue in other halls and offices and reverberate through our lives.

Undergraduates have as much trouble thinking of discourse differently. In a preservice education course at Cornell we have students conduct interviews designed to probe another person's understanding of some topic in science or mathematics. My undergraduate preservice science teachers labor all semester to learn the different mode of discourse needed for good interviewing. Initially, it is simply hard for them to ask the real questions clinical interviews require, questions that are not gratuitous or superficial. It is also hard for them to listen to answers, and use those answers to formulate further questions. Once they practice these processes, my students try to develop questions about everyday events that could tease out interviewees' real thoughts rather than rotely memorized phrases. My students had no previous experience at discourse directed to finding out someone else's ideas and found it somehow improper to question and listen intently. The interviewees, also college students, were not accustomed to expressing their own views about commonplace phenomena. Both interviewer and interviewee felt pressure either to give or elicit the accepted view or "right answer" they all felt should have been learned in earlier science classes. The pressure to find "the right answer" plagued my students all semester. I would read one interview and feel the student had mastered the interview process, only to be disappointed by the next interview in which the student would criticize the "wrong" ideas held by the interviewee. I think that, by the end of the semester, students were beginning to reach the views I hoped they would. Their erratic progress is one more indication of the meandering development of new understandings.

If the elementary science teaching encouraged by these authors is to occur, the physical arrangements of classrooms must also change. Elementary classrooms in which pupils pursue science projects will be messier, noisier, and take up more space than classrooms relying on more typical approaches. Materials that need to be explored have to be arranged throughout a classroom, a process that will inevitably create disarray. Systematic investigation and experimentation with materials will continue the apparent disorder. The processes that pupils will be learning are not chaotic, but the physical arrangements in classrooms may look chaotic. An obvious point, perhaps, but for teachers evaluated by an administrator who favors order above all else, order exemplified by desks in rows, clean shelves, and children in their seats, the point is not at all trivial. Hence, there is the need for elementary school administrators to understand the underlying order of this approach to learning science.

Some administrative circles are urging that principals learn to use clinical supervision, a process that requires them to provide more guidance to teachers rather than just evaluating them. Teachers hoping to implement some of the ideas in these chapters need help. A principal who does not understand the aims and processes will be less than no help, he or she will be a detriment.

If we take seriously the notion of teaching presented in these chapters, teachers will be researchers in their own classrooms, investigating phenomena with their students and learning with them, and also investigating the processes of investigation going on in the classrooms. Teachers will practice as professionals in this kind of science teaching. This professionalism will not be the result of the number of credit hours taken, the salary or specialized role in the school, but the result of continual investigation of classroom practice. Teacher education must support teachers' development by providing numerous occasions for teachers and prospective teachers to practice as professionals, able to monitor, evaluate, and revise their efforts.

Traditional grading procedures, for example, must be carefully examined and revised to contribute to the development of the requisite abilities. A colleague of mine, Bill Carlsen, is not relying on usual assignments and exams to establish student's grades. He gives regular and widely varied assignments throughout the semester and evaluates them meticulously. The course grade, however, is based on a portfolio of work selected and presented by each student. The student has the responsibility to select and explain those artifacts that he or she feels represents his or her work in the course. Students struggle with this project, feel confused, want more direction, but learn.

CONCLUSION

A fundamental assumption shared by these authors is that the notion of science held by too many elementary school educators is mistaken, based on a lack of appreciation or understanding of the social and experiential elements of constructing science knowledge and the extent to which scientific knowledge is tentative and open to question. Those holding this mistaken view of science teaching regard it as the imparting of facts and principles. When students and their teachers do not know how the knowledge in science is constructed and justified, they can easily assume they have no ability or power to do science themselves or to challenge the findings of science. These authors illustrate how elementary science can, and must, begin with explorations of events in the everyday world so that students learn how to investigate scientifically and thereby form the basis for later learning of sophisticated science concepts.

The fundamental beliefs about the nature of science and of children held by these authors shape their view of learning, of curriculum, of teachers' and students' roles. Elementary science does not require elaborate materials or texts. We are surrounded by phenomena that can be investigated systematically. The needed science curriculum is a compendium of projects of interest to children of different ages that can be fruitfully investigated and suggestions about how students get involved in these investigations. Teachers can help students learn how to conduct studies, communicate their thinking and direct and evaluate their learning. Students can be the curious and active creatures they naturally are.

To return to the initial image, the following chapters help us to know what it would be like to explore various parts of the "Grand Canyon," the reconceptualized image of teaching science and teaching about science. The stories told by these author/explorers open up parts of the Canyon to us without trivializing it. The stories told in these chapters tell of the magnificence and wonder of pupils' learning and invite us to become involved. We learn that this involvement will not be easy, that our own travels in the Canyon will require much effort, but we are assured the endeavor is worth all the care and energy we can give to it.

REFERENCES

Ehrlich G., (1985). *The solace of open spaces*. New York: Penguin Books.

Mayher, J.S., Lester, N., & Pradl, G.M. (1983). *Learning to write, writing to learn*. Upper Montclair, NJ: Boynton/Cook.

Miller, J. (1987). Teachers' emerging texts: The empowering potential of writing in-service. In J. Smyth (Ed.), *Educating teachers: Changing the nature or pedagogical knowledge* (pp. 161–178). London: Falmer Press.

Moffett, J. (1968). *Teaching the universe of discourse*. Boston: Houghton Mifflin.

Moffett, J. (1985). Hidden impediments to improving English teaching. *Phi Delta Kappan, 67*, 51–57.

Willis, P. (1978). *Learning to labour*. Westmead: Saxon House.

2

Opening the World

Eleanor Duckworth
Harvard Graduate School of Education

It started on the first day of school, when Carla brought in a monarch chrysalis, whose metamorphosis we followed with rapt attention. The idea of metamorphosis took on new dimensions as the children began to find other larvae—such as maggots, caterpillars, and apple worms—and bring them to school to see what they would hatch into. Many of them never changed into anything, but the children were interested in finding out what they would have hatched into, had they made it. Some of the cocoons which were spun in our room we kept all year, because we thought perhaps they needed to winter over and would hatch in the spring. (They didn't.)

Different things were interesting to different people. Some of the children were captivated by the notion that familiar insects, such as butterfiles, moths and flies, grew out of these wormy looking things. Most everyone wanted to know how it happened, how the larva "knew" to become a butterfly or moth or whatever. Closely aligned to this was the desire to see the process in action . . . Then, from early on, there were children who got interested in the patterns.

(Schwartz, 1986, p. 22)

From this opening, Ellen Schwartz, a public school teacher in Vermont, describes a year of work with her first and second graders, under the title, *An Over-repeating Story.* The story ranged through natural

21

science, physical science, math, art, and literature. (It was the literary element that prompted one child to coin the phrase Schwartz used as her title; the children came to use the phrase to refer to patterns they saw in story lines, insect lives, and geometrical designs.) Children brought in "anything they thought might be an insect" (p. 23), and, in addition to crickets, grasshoppers, ants, centipedes, and spiders, they started to bring bits of bees' and wasps' nests. This expanded their set of investigations to the structure of the nests. In the books they consulted about bees, the cells in the nests were drawn as hexagons. "The children . . . were puzzled by it, because our real nest sections didn't look like they were made up of hexagons. Our cells looked more like rough circles. There was a question raised here, a dissatisfaction: Why doesn't it look like the pictures in the books? How can we know if they're really hexagons?" (p. 24).

Hexagons were known to the children, because of their work with pattern blocks and altair designs. This was one way that patterns were present in their work. Another way that patterns came in was through one child's interest in crystals: the children collected them, made a crystal "museum," grew crystals, examined them under a microscope, read books about them. One child found pictures of snow crystals, and these, in turn, took them right back to hexagons. One snowflake picture led them to build, with their pattern blocks, a 12-sided polygon, and some of the children were intrigued to find that, inside such a shape, patterns could be found 1, 2, 3, 6, or 12 times. Why those numbers, they wondered, and some of their explorations led to the factors of 12. Other children appreciated, above all, the beauty of the patterns.

Interest returned to the bees' nests, and the children decided to open the one undamaged nest (a hornet's nest, in fact) they had been admiring since the autumn. Inside they themselves saw that each layer was roughly hexagonal in shape. This time, in contrast to the earlier encounter with imprecise hexagonal cell shapes, the children had greater familiarity with hexagons. They explored them still further with their pattern blocks, and came to understand how those layers could be seen to approximate hexagons.

The story had not stopped repeating. The seventh and eighth graders put up in the school hallway a display of "Islamic designs" that they had made. The similarities with their own patterns intrigued the first and second graders enough to invite two older children to tell them about their designs and about Islam. This visit led to further pattern making, with the additional use of compasses.

"There isn't a real ending to this story," wrote Schwartz. "The school ended and so we had to stop" (p. 26).

What I want to say about [it] . . . has something to do with science and a lot to do with time. I never intended to do "a unit on hexagons" (which this wasn't), or even to connect crystals and bees. . . . I'm not particularly concerned that they can't define an insect or crystal, or verbalize the importance of the hexagon. I *am* concerned that they have the opportunity and encouragement to return to such themes in the future, because, as this one year has shown me, it is in the returning that understandings begin to take form and deepen. (p. 27)

I have started with this teacher's story (whose entirety, by the way, is far more fascinating than this abridgement) because it exemplifies the inherent appeal of good science education for young children. It would be hard for anyone to question the value of the activities described here. Someone might question whether these activities took too much time away from preparing for reading and arithmetic tests. But nobody is likely to think that these activities are not worthwhile. Moreover, they seem to be full of interest—not only for the children, but also (and above all, in this account in which the children's voices are not themselves heard) for the teacher. And, speaking for myself, for the reader.

It also exemplifies the rewards, for a teacher, of being open to paths unanticipated. And it exemplifies this without apparently requiring a teacher with extensive science knowledge.

The question that this chapter addresses is: How can we bring about more such studies in elementary schools? What might enable other teachers to open the world in that way to their elementary school students? I would like to address this question by describing my work with teachers. But first, I would like to mention three interrelated obstacles to such teaching.

In my view one of the greatest obstacles is the fierce concentration on standardized tests of reading and arithmetic. It is not a concentration on reading and arithmetic per se that gets in the way. Schwartz's story would be wholly appropriate in a class that was concentrating on reading and arithmetic. The theme came from literature, the children read books about bees and crystals, the geometrical patterns led into factors and multiples of numbers. But the concentration in schools today is not on reading and arithmetic. It is on *standardized tests* of reading and arithmetic, which is quite a different matter. None of the work described here could be appreciated on a standardized test. My point here is that including science in the elementary curriculum does not interfere with the teaching of reading and arithmetic. On the contrary, it complements and supports this teaching. What it does interfere with is practicing for standardized tests of reading and arithmetic, which take little account of the long term or the broad scope of learning. It is the grip of these standardized tests that so limits the ways teachers and children spend their time in elementary schools. One, among many, of the victims is science education.

A second, not unrelated, factor is that in most school systems, teachers are seen as cogs in a bureaucratic machine, not as professionals who go about their work with intelligence. As functionaries, teachers are to carry out instructions, to do what they are told. If science teaching is to be done, it is to be done in spite of the teachers, by narrowly specifying each question, demonstration, finding, and conclusion. On the contrary, I believe we must demand teachers' intelligence, interest, and thoughtfulness. No program for elementary science education can flourish independent of the intelligent participation of teachers.

As Claryce Evans (1986), a public school administrator concerned about science teaching in elementary schools has pointed out, a third factor lies behind these two: the commonly held view of what constitutes knowledge. Knowledge, according to this view, is held by somebody authoritative, and it needs to be transmitted to the student. It follows that important knowledge, once identified, should be ordered from easy to difficult, and printed in textbooks, or vouchsafed to teachers, who can then explain. Children are to practice repeating the knowledge, and are to be tested to see whether they repeat it correctly or incorrectly.

I believe that Evans has indeed characterized a widely held view of the nature of knowledge. It contrasts strikingly, however, with the views presented in this book, of which I would like to underline two premises. The first is one which David Hawkins develops eloquently: The subject matter of science is the world itself, with all its fascination and perplexity. Knowledge found in books can help lead a person into this subject matter, but it is not the subject matter itself.

Second, as Henriques urges, knowledge necessarily belongs to the knower. The world may well exist on its own, but knowledge of it, however adequate or inadequate, belongs to each of us. The knowledge that a teacher must be concerned with is that of the *student*. It is this knowledge that he or she wants to see further developed, *and* this is the knowledge the teacher has to work with. Learners construct further knowledge by modifying that which they have already.

These two premises give us an idea of what it means to know something that departs radically from the view that Evans brings to our attention. First, we want to acquaint children with the world itself, with all of its fascination. Second, we must start and end with the students' knowledge rather than someone else's, no matter how authoritative.

In my work, I have paid most attention to this third obstacle, the understanding of the nature of knowledge. The bulk of this chapter is concerned with my work with teachers, and its influence on how they think and feel about their own and the children's knowledge of science.

WORKING WITH TEACHERS

In my work with teachers, I try to do two things:

1. I try to engage teachers with the habits and peculiarities of the material world, the real subject matter of science. I think it is important, as Easley does, that teachers who find science an alien world come to feel more comfortable in it. I try to help them feel at ease with at least some parts of this world, so they appreciate it, and feel that they want and are able to find out more about it. I think it is also important for teachers who are relatively at ease with science to be reintroduced to areas with which they have some familiarity: to discover that even in areas with which they thought they were familiar, they can be taken by surprise, and that it is the surprises that hold the potential for further learning.

I want teachers to appreciate the fact that knowledge of the material world is both accessible and complex. These two qualities may seem contradictory or incompatible. Accessible could be understood as simple and complex as inaccessible. But it is the complexity that makes things accessible. It is the complexity that takes away the unique privilege of the "expert" to know all that can be known, in the only way it can be known. Someone can "know" what textbooks contain, and still not be able to fathom what is happening in some particular instance. It is the complexity that allows each of us to know differently and validly, that is, which makes this world accessible to each of us.

2. As they become engaged with the material world, I also try to have them look at themselves and each other as learners of science: what gets them interested, what they think they know, what they do about what they don't know, how other people's ideas affect them, how they feel as they are learning. At the same time, I have them look closely at children who are engaged in learning about the material world: what *they* know and seem to know, what gets them interested, what they say about what they know, and what they do with it.

I introduce a topic one might say innocently, in the sense that I try to convey an assumption that it is straightforward and accessible. I start with some phenomenon, rather than a title—I ask them to try to make an odd-shaped piece of cardboard hang from a straightpin in some specified position, for example, rather than announcing that we are about to study the center of gravity. I want the students to find that there are complexities they had never dreamt of, without having the study become less accessible. Elsewhere, I have written an account of eight sessions during which a group of teachers explored sinking and floating phenomena (see Duckworth, 1986). Other groups of teachers have spent equally long periods exploring balances, pendulums, or time-measuring machines. Sometimes, however, we leave a topic fairly quickly. Because my overall purpose is not in having them learn about a particular topic, but in succeeding in engaging them in some investigation, my case is not furthered by urging them through some activities that have not caught their interest.

If, as they work, the students run out of ideas, or are stumped by a phenomenon, and cannot think how to go about understanding it, my major effort is directed toward finding some further activity to propose, perhaps some variations on what they have already done, even if I have little idea of what might happen. I usually find that in this continued activity something attracts their interest, and they start following ideas of their own again.

I give a few examples here of engaging teachers or prospective teachers with this accessible, complex world.

Siphons

One group of undergraduates in a science methods course used the available materials to make a siphon. Once they had made it work, they were ready to leave it for something else. I tried to keep them with it, finding new aspects. I put a question to them that had been asked by some children. In the set-up in Fig. 2.1, as long as both siphons keep running does the middle container always maintain the same level?

They realized they did not need to set up a double siphon system. What they needed to do was to explore what factors made one siphon

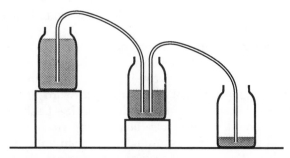

FIG. 2.1.

flow faster than another. One group changed the diameter of one of the tubes, and found that a wider tube moved the water faster than a narrower tube. Another group suggested changing the heights of the containers. They went about this by looking at the effect of changing the height of the water in a container, with the following set-up. The first time, they simply filled the upper jar, and siphoned the water out into the lower jar, until it reached a pre-established mark on the lower jar. They timed how long this took. The second time, as the upper jar emptied, they kept filling it again, while the siphon was still at work— which had the effect that the water level in the upper jar was, on average, higher the second time than the first time. Timing this one also, they found that the water reached the pre-established mark on the lower jar more quickly than in the first trial.

Other questions arose. Was it the absolute height of the water, compared to the height of the other container, or was it the depth of the water in the upper container? Which of these, for example, would fill the lower container faster? (See Fig. 2.2.)

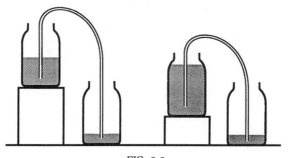

FIG. 2.2.

They found that the left one did.

Did the depth of the tube in the upper jar make a difference? (See Fig. 2.3.)

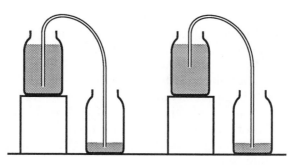

FIG. 2.3.

Did the simple length of the tube make a difference? (See Fig. 2.4.)

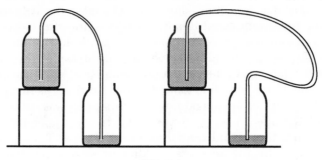

FIG. 2.4.

Carrying out many such experiments, they established that the only thing that mattered was the difference in height between the water level in the upper jar and the water level in the lower jar.

Then there was also the question of whether the lower tube had to be in a container of water at the bottom. If it is not, but is simply pouring into the air, then what happens?

One experiment they devised that answered a number of their questions at once was the following (see Fig. 2.5).

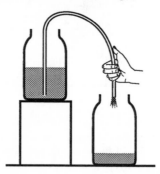

FIG. 2.5.

The lower the low end of the tube, the faster the water flowed. As the tube was raised, the flow slowed until the end was opposite—not the upper end of the tube, but the surface of the water in the upper container. At that point, the flow stopped.

After this much familiarity with what siphons actually do, we found ourselves in a state of perplexity over the question of how fast the water is flowing in different parts of the tube at the same time! Some thought that if it came out at a certain speed, it must be flowing at that speed throughout. Others thought, referring specifically to the experiment just described, that in the higher parts of the tube, the water must be flowing more slowly. This did not seem very convincing to most of us until someone suggested the following. If, while water was flowing through it, you cut the tube, the water would now flow more slowly. But how could the water "know," as it were, that the tube had been cut? Would this slower flow not indicate that that was its speed of flow past that point even when the tube was longer?

Throughout this discussion, of course, we were drawing on what we thought we knew about how siphons worked. "Air pressure" and "water pressure" had been featured in the explanations. But at this point no such words helped make sense of the phenomena. We started talking in more ordinary terms. The most common way of talking about what was happening was that the water in the top jar was pushing down, pushing some water up into the tube (perhaps helped by air pressure, nobody was sure about that; do siphons work in a vacuum?) But this, we now realized, did not help us figure out how the water would "know" how fast to run out of the tube. As the water, and/or air, is pushing the water into the upper end of the tube, how does it "know" what is going on at the other end of the tube? One student proposed a different way to think about it: The water is being pulled down out of the lower end of the tube. Because it is full of water, and submerged in water at the upper end, it has to pull water with it, in order to pour out the bottom. Did this help us any more than the other way of thinking about it? We weren't sure. But we certainly knew a lot more about siphons than we had before. And we knew that saying "air pressure" or "water pressure" did not help us understand.

The Blind Spot

This same group spent some time exploring aspects of their own bodies—comparisons of finger lengths and toe lengths, proportions between parts of their bodies, locating direction of sound, with one ear or two ears. The particular investigation I discuss here was exploring the blind spot of the eye.

I had prepared a number of 3 × 5 cards with an x and a dot, in the following manner (Fig. 2.6):

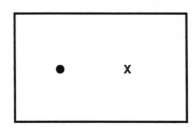

FIG. 2.6.

I asked them to close one eye, look at the x, and move the card closer and farther away from their face. Some of them soon found that the dot disappeared when the card was at a certain distance from the eye. As others tried to replicate this finding, they came to realize that, in order to experience the phenomenon, they had to pay attention to the relationship between the orientation of the card and the eye that was open or closed. Before long, all of them could manipulate the card in such a way as to make the dot disappear.

They became intrigued with this phenomenon, and sought ways to explore it further. The most common interpretation was that this indicated the edge of the field of vision. Someone suggested making the dot bigger. Now it did not wholly disappear. Moreover, one of them noticed that as the card moved closer to and farther from her eye, she could see the large dot first start to disappear from one side, and then start to reappear from that same side. This cast a lot of doubt on the idea that this was an indicator of the edge of the field of vision.

Christiane suggested drawing a vertical line in place of the dot. There was disagreement about whether or not the middle of the line disappeared. She then suggested putting a small horizontal line in the middle of the vertical (see Fig. 2.7).

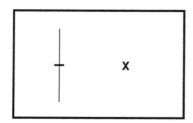

FIG. 2.7.

This time, the small horizontal line definitely disappeared; but the vertical did not seem to be broken. This came as a surprise, and led to the most interesting insight of all a little later.

By now they were talking of a "black spot," or an "empty spot." Their first tendency was to locate this at the the outside corner of the visible part of the eye. With further thought, they placed it on the retina, and on the side toward the nose. I contributed my understanding of its origin.

One of them then suggested looking at a fixed place on a black card, instead of a white one, to see if we could tell what exact shape the empty spot is. She was thinking that because we had so far made black dots and lines disappear, with white spots left in their place, the empty spot would always make black disappear, leaving white in its place. Christiane said, it wouldn't work that way: You wouldn't then see a white spot; it would be filled in. And that then raised a wonderful question: How does the eye know what to fill in the blind spot with—if what it is looking at is not a uniform white or black card?

We did not have a black paper. But as we tried to think what to do next, someone came up with a postcard picture of a very ornate flamboyant gothic cathedral. To see what the blind spot did with this, we would choose one spot on the card as the fixed x and another as the spot we would make disappear into the blind spot. What would be in its place? The spot we chose to make disappear was a particularly ornate spire. It turned out that we could indeed tell when we did not see it any more. And in its place was more flamboyant gothic decoration! There was no white spot, no recognizable disturbance of the picture. That part of the picture, where the spire had been, was slightly out of focus, because it was not in the center of our field, but as far as we could tell, it was the same there as anywhere in that region of the card—a lot of decoration.

I had already known how much of vision is constructed by our minds. But this manifestation of what our eye and mind together manage to do in order to present us with a coherent image was one I had never encountered in my time as a psychology student. It was a dramatic introduction to that idea for these student teachers. And it came to them as their own idea, from their own explorations, as they rendered more complex a phenomenon that is usually considered a simple demonstration. (See chapter 4 for some history of thinking about vision.)

Mirrors

In a third example, an extended one, I would like to give an idea of how such a class goes—the questions that arise, the ways the students express their ideas, the ways they respond to each other's ideas, my own responses. The subject of study is mirrors. I had begun with a version of the question Hawkins (1978) drew attention to in his classic paper, "Critical Barriers to Science Learning." There were about 50 students in the class, seated in the room as represented in Fig. 2.8. John and Fernando were seated as indicated. Hawkins' question would have been, if the wall marked A–C–B were a mirror, where on that mirror would John look in order to see Fernando?

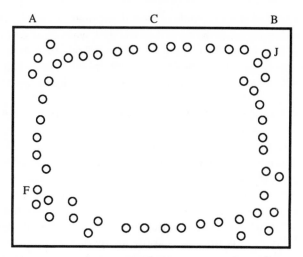

FIG. 2.8.

I have asked the question in that form, but the way we check our predictions is with a single smallish mirror, placed in one position. I have found that students consider the placement of one small mirror to be a different question from the position on a mirror wall. So this time I asked, instead, where on the wall should we place this mirror so that John can see Fernando when he looks in it? I include here the dialogue through the first three predictions.

Fernando: I'm not supposed to see him?

Duckworth: That wasn't in the question one way or the other. It was so John can see you. So. Jane has an idea.

Jane: My idea would be to put it straight in a line with Fernando, right on that wall [at A] . . . So that if John can see that mirror, then he'll see him.

Wendy: I was thinking the exact opposite. I thought the same thing you did at first, right over here. Then I thought maybe the closer it is to John, [hesitantly] the more he could see him. I was thinking maybe right next to John on the wall [at B].

Duckworth: [in an attempt to get her thoughts more explicit, for myself and for everyone else]—Uh, because the closer it is to him, the more he'll—, . . . he would see the whole room then.

Wendy: I'm not sure how much, but I think he would see a lot

more than he would trying to see the mirror all the way
down here [at A].

Duckworth: OK.

Barbara: If you put it right in front of him, then he won't see
anything but himself. . . . You have to put it at some kind
of angle so he can see to the side.

Wendy: Well you don't always just look in front of you. . . . Well
it depends on I guess how much he was allowed to move
his head. If he was looking at it straight or if he was
looking at it into maybe the right side of the mirror?
Looking in the right side of the mirror maybe he'd be able
to see this [Fernando's] side of the room?

Beverly: I think it would be the middle [C] that would give him a
wide spread. Because . . . then it could stretch this far.
[She gestures from John in the direction of Fernando.]
And if it was there [A] he might not be able to see the
mirror on the wall, which is flat. There would be less
chance. . . . And it should be slightly higher than seat
height.

Duckworth: Slightly higher than seat height, on the wall half way.

These were the first three ideas. There were others, and a lot of
interesting discussion. We did not check out any of the predictions
right then, but instead they broke up into small groups with mirrors,
and did whatever they thought would be helpful to them to figure out
that prediction. In a later class, we did hear reports of what people
had done in that time, and in the meantime, at home, and we carried
out as a group some of the explorations that seemed of greatest
general interest. By that time I believe the following generalizations
would have been agreed to by everyone: If John and Fernando were
equally distant from the wall, then the mirror should be halfway
between them, at the height of their heads; if one of them was closer to
the wall, then the mirror should be closer to him. They also agreed
that if one of them could see another, then they could both see each
other.

One of the moments of greatest astonishment in this class belonged
to Jane (who had made the first prediction in the earlier class). While
the rest of the class watched, a small group of people was working.
There was a moment when Lisa, Marie, and Nona were arranged as
sketched here, and, although Lisa and Nona could see each other,
Marie could see neither of them (see Fig. 2.9).

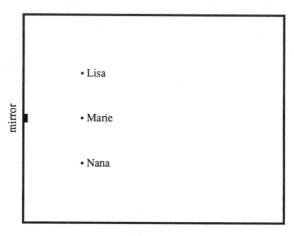

FIG. 2.9.

Jane was flabbergasted. She wrote about it this way:

> I remember that at the moment I realized this I felt physically odd. . . . It was . . . what I imagine seeing a ghost must be like. I felt like I was in a science fiction story, but this was real. At the end of class [we gathered] around a mirror on the floor. . . . We all saw something that was different than what everyone else saw. This made it clear to me that what was bothering me was a *real* phenomenon.

> I could see that a mirror could hold different images at once, but I could not accept it deep down. I knew it but didn't believe it . . .

> I have learned a lot from being bothered by this aspect of mirrors. Most importantly, it pointed out to me the fundamental difference between mirrors and . . . a painting, say.

In fact, when each person found a different person in the mirror on the floor, many others joined Jane in her astonishment: How could they all fit? How was it that they did not get in each other's way? The idea of image-in-mirror-as-picture-on-mirror seemed widespread.

The next time we looked at mirrors in class, small groups worked on questions of their choice. Some people were still working on versions of the original question. Some were working on what happens to what you see as a result of being closer to or farther from a mirror. I raised a new question, with some small hand mirrors I had brought: Could I see my whole face in such a mirror (placed flush against a vertical wall)? And a related question: How big a mirror do you need to see your whole self? I had also brought some flashlights and some string, without proposing any particular question to investigate with them.

At the end of that class, there had scarcely been time to find out what people had done. We had discussed only the experiments of people who were trying to figure out how big a mirror you need to see your whole face or your whole self. Because most of them had started bytrying to decide how far away to put the mirror, in order to start, the question found itself transformed into: What happens to the size of your image as you move closer to or farther from the mirror? Some people had found the size changed, others had found it didn't.

The class described in greater detail here was the next one, a reporting session. Glenn started by describing an experiment he had done at home in the meantime. He had held a yardstick beside his face, walked closer to and farther from the mirror, and found that he could always see the same number of inches. He reported that his mirror was about 4 inches high, and that he could always see about 7 inches of yardstick-by-his-face. After people had asked a number of questions about details of his technique, I asked for other reports.

> Jean: I wear glasses for distance, right? Last week when Ruth and I were upstairs—she didn't think this was amazing, but I did—we were in the long hall, we were upstairs, and she was walking back further and further away, and I was holding the mirror right up there, and as she walked further back she got fuzzier and fuzzier. . . . The image, right, in the mirror. Only I was really close to the mirror.

[Several voices—Oh!]

> Jean: And then when I put my glasses on, there she was in focus.

[There was a considerable number of exclamations, including, "Neat!" "She was fuzzier in the mirror?" "That's wierd!" and a request for her to say it over again.]

> Jean: OK, here's the mirror, practically on my nose. So there's no problem with me seeing the mirror because it's right in front of my face. But I'm looking at Ruth in the mirror who's going further and further away, walking back, you know, the length of this building, right? As she gets further away she gets fuzzier and fuzzier to me looking at her in the mirror!

[This time there was a loud wave of astonished sounds.]

Ricky: Have you ever driven without your glasses on?

Jean: I have to say I have, yeah. (Loud peals of laughter.)

Ricky: Do you think you'd have the same thing looking in your rear-view mirror at a car behind you?

Jean: I didn't ever notice it before, but now I noticed it, yeah. Headlights, you know, whether they're big and fuzzy or whether they're tight.

[Jane made a connection between this and the source of her great astonishment in the previous class.]

Jane: One of the things that have really been bothering me about the mirrors was that we could see all these different images? It was like, what happens to the image, that you could see? And there must be something . . . something about the nature of something that's far away, that's still the same when it's reflected off of a mirror. Does that make sense?

Ginny: It doesn't seem as though it should be, though.

Jean: I know. I couldn't believe it, I really couldn't.

Fran: I want to go try it.

Maggie
to Ruth: Why didn't you think it was amazing?

Ruth: Because I thought it made sense . . . If she turned around and looked at me I would look fuzzy to her, so why should it be any different because she's looking in a mirror? It's still the same—she has to see through the same distance.

[Kathryn referred back to the mirror-as-picture in a different way from Jane.]

Kathryn: It must be, what we were saying before, how the mirror isn't a painting. So we're thinking of it, if it's close up it's like a painting, we should be able to see it. But I guess that must be a trap there.

Sally: This is sort of related, I think. I tried to measure my image in the mirror. Or I was doing it with another person, so I would stand back about 8 feet and the other person would hold the ruler up to the mirror, and measure my image across . . . which was smaller than my image really is, and this was a big mirror. So the image in the mirror was, say, 8 inches across, whereas I'm really, maybe, 13 inches across. Does everyone understand what I'm saying? [She was interested in whether things are the same size in a mirror as they are in real life. This was actually a part of what Glenn had reported—in a 4-inch mirror he had seen 7 inches—but she did not make any reference back to him.]

Elsa: [casting some doubt on Sally's finding, not to mention Glenn's, but referring to neither of them]—I was going to say that might have something to do with the quality or type of mirror, because think of a fun house, you can look fatter or much skinnier, depending on a wave or a ripple in the glass itself. I think that if you had the perfect mirror, that you would probably be as big as you are in the mirror.

Audrey: Is that true?

Elsa: I'm not sure. I don't know.

Duckworth: [not noticing that the real problem here would be to figure out whether we had a perfect mirror]—It's a good thing to try.

Brenda: It seems as though what you were doing, though, was still different from what you [Glenn] did.

Sally: Yes, it is different.

Brenda: You [Glenn] were measuring, if I heard it, how much of that yardstick was visible, and you [Sally] were saying, how big is my image, but not, how much of me is visible. [This did help to differentiate the two concerns, though she still does not seem to realize that Glenn's findings had included both.] . . . With the yardstick in the mirror, take a *real* yardstick, and see if the inches are bigger or smaller.

Sally: Well that was my point. Is an inch an inch when you put it in the mirror.

Margaret: [still concerned with whether the size of the image you see of yourself changes as you change your distance from the mirror]—If you cut a mirror exactly in the outline of your body, to size, and you backed up, you would see a change in size.

Duckworth: That's do-able, too, by drawing an outline. In fact, you could draw an outline of some part of you, on a mirror, as much as the mirror will take.

Carl: [returning to the question of whether an inch is an inch when you put it in the mirror]—I was just wondering, you know, if you look at a road, in the distance, and it comes together, why would that not be at work with a mirror? I mean, if the ruler is far away, why would it not look smaller even in the mirror, than it would if it was right in front of your face?

Brenda: Except you can't always—I really don't think, I haven't figured this out yet, but I really don't think you can see more of yourself if you go way way back.

Carl: I don't think you can, either. I think—. You know, but in terms of, is an inch an inch when it's right there in front of you or if it's reflected in a mirror which is ten feet away, I don't think the answer's going to be the same.

We turned to another question now. The question another pair had pursued was, do you see more or less behind you if you are closer to or farther from the mirror. We held a mirror at a distance from Jessica, and she described all that she could see behind her.

Duckworth: OK, Jessica can see the woman behind her, and the blond woman, and Ed. OK, here we go. [The mirror is carried closer to Jessica.]

Jessica: Now I can see more people. A lot more.

Duckworth: I don't know if that's considered a critical experiment, if you take Jessica's word for it, or what we do with that, but . . . has anybody got contradicting evidence to that? That is, you get closer to the mirror and you see less?

Shirley: [returning yet again to the previous question] It depends on the size mirror. With a small hand mirror you can see more of your hand [she meant more of your face] at this distance. When it's up here then you only see your nose, your mouth—

Duckworth: That's the big question we were just discussing.

Shirley: Yeah. So that's what I'm saying.

Brian: I don't agree with that.

Harvey: I don't agree with that.

Duckworth: Some people don't agree with that.

Harvey: I think you can see the same amount of your face when you have it right here as when [it's farther away] . . .

Shirley: I mean, your face doesn't shrink. You can see your hair [when the mirror is farther away]—I mean, you can't see your hair [when it's close]—

Harvey: No, I can see the exact same amount of my face.

Jeff: I did that last week. Cause I had just a little round one, and I was going like this [moving the mirror closer to and farther from his face]. While people were talking last week I was going like that. And I couldn't believe it either, but I could see the same amount of my face when I went like this [closer and farther].

Duckworth: Anybody else want to check that out?

[I handed out a number of small mirrors then, and lot of people experimented. After a few minutes, we took up the discussion again.]

Edith: [finally putting together Sally's question with this persistent one] Something that makes a little more sense to me now is that I found, um, against my expectations, that if I hold it here and if I hold it here [closer to or farther from her face] I see the same amount of my face. *But*, when it's closer here it *looks* as though it's bigger. Because of the way your eyes adjust to distance. Because here maybe it's twice as far away. So the reflection looks smaller.

Nick: But the whole mirror should look smaller.

Edith: Yeah, well it does.

Abbie: It's true.

[Quite a lot of interested chatter. This being essentially a reporting session, however, in a very large group, I moved on.]

Duckworth: Since not everybody has mirrors, I think we'll move on from this. . . . So what happened with flashlights?

Danielle: I thought I had the mirrors figured out, and then, we did something with the flashlight. I forget what we did. We moved in? As we moved in the size of the reflection got smaller?

Paul: Uh, got larger. When we were way back in the corner, it was round and small [the spot of light that hit the ceiling, after bouncing off the mirror] . . . Yeah, when the flashlight gets closer to the mirror, it dispersed the rays at a wider angle.

Duckworth: So if you had a flashlight close to the mirror, it had a great big circle up there.

Paul: Yeah, huge.

Danielle: And then when we moved around on the side, though, didn't it change, too?

Paul: Not the size, though.
Michael: Only the dot moved, along the wall.
Paul: Yeah, it did the same, it proved the same thing that
         someone else was working on, I mean, that we had done
         before, about the angles staying the same.
Michael: Yeah . . . If I was in one corner, the opposite corner, the
         dot would be back in the other corner. But as I moved in
         toward the center of the wall, it would come close to me
         (see Fig 2.10).

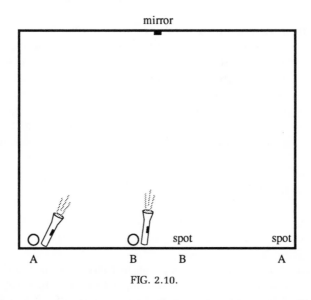

FIG. 2.10.

[I asked for other flashlight experiments people had done.]

Fernando: We were worried about the reality of the mirror, like what
           appeared to be on your right was on the left, and all that
           kind of stuff. So what we did, we pointed the flashlight
           from the top, and the light, the reflection was at the
           bottom. And when we pointed the flashlight at the
           bottom, going to the mirror, straight at the same position,
           the reflection was at the top.

[Note that it was significant to Fernando that the light could hit the
very same spot on the mirror, but bounce off somewhere else. We
turned off the lights and tried this ourselves. After we had confirmed
what Fernando had said, Neil picked up on Danielle's issue.]

Neil: Eleanor, can you move the flashlight closer to the mirror and then further away from the mirror on the same angle? [I do it.] So the beam does spread out when you get closer to the mirror.

Joseph: The spot stays at the same place. [Various interested acknowledgments of this.] That's what the theory would make it. [More agreement.]

Duckworth: What's the theory?

Joseph: [hesitantly] As long as you're walking . . .

Fernando: —in the same angle—

Kathryn: —in the same line, you could see the other person (see Fig. 2.11).

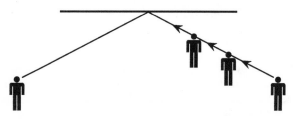

FIG. 2.11.

Neil: Oh I see, I see what you mean.

Joseph: That's what we found. We found that real early on.

Neil: [going back to his original question of the size of the spot of light] I was wondering if there was a correlation between the amount of light you could see spread out on the ceiling, and how much you can see behind you when you get closer to the mirror. Do you see what I'm saying?

Duckworth: So what we've learned is that Jessica saw more when the mirror got closer to her, and the light spot was bigger when the flashlight was closer. I'm not sure what they have to do with each other . . .

Neil: I'm not either . . .

Duckworth: —but it's worth thinking about. [We do not pursue this right now]. . . .

Jacqueline: . . . We shone the light into the mirror, at an angle, and . . . another person stood where the spot of light was reflecting, and we wanted to see if it was the same angle that we could see each other, and it was.

[I propose that we do this. With the overhead light off, Jacqueline shines the flashlight into the mirror, and a spot of light lights up Stuart. Then they turn the overhead lights back on again, and Jacqueline looks in the mirror.]

Jacqueline: Yeah, I can see him. I don't know if he can see me in the tiny mirror way way away. I can see him. It seems like it's the same angle we're dealing with . . .

This excerpt gives an idea of the range of questions that come up, the variety of different things there are to do, how hard people work at trying to understand each other, how complicated seemingly simple ideas really are, and how engrossing ordinary phenomena can be. I would like to complement that excerpt with the following one from one student's final paper.

Richard began moving the mirror and then he asked me first to fix my eyes on one spot on the mirror while he held it still. I think this has something to do with—eeek!—vectors! But I don't know what vectors are. There is some connection, though, with the movement of my eyes in the angles of the mirror, but what?

Later that night, tired and not really thinking about much, I made a small, but significant, discovery. The journal entry describes this:

"I was lying on my couch looking out the sliding glass doors that lead to the balcony. I saw part of the living room reflected in the doors and I recalled that I often use the doors as a mirror but only at night when it's dark outside and the lights are on in the living room . . . Then I noticed something really strange. In the doorway to the bathroom it was completely black. There is no window in the bathroom and the light was off, but reflected in the living room sliding doors was the oddest thing: in the area where the darkness of the bathroom door should be I saw instead the leaves of the tree that is outside the balcony!

"I went into the bathroom and turned on the light. When I came back into the living room the tree was 'gone'! and in its place I could see the part of the lighted bathroom reflected in the balcony door. So! there must be light in order for a mirror to reflect. Now I must find out what it is that the light does."

It was a week later during an exploration of the mirror with my long-suffering daughter that we discovered together, by shining a flashlight into a mirror so that the light shone on the actual objects we aimed the light at, that the light bent.

"The light bends," we cried like the most triumphant of physicists. (Brooks, 1986, pp. 13–14)

TEACHERS' RESPONSES TO THIS WORK

There are two ways I would like to present the teachers' responses to this approach to science. One is through quotes from their writing about the experience. The other is through descriptions of their work with children.

Quotes From Teachers' Writing

I have chosen quotes that particularly address the commonly held view of knowledge and curriculum, as clarified earlier by Evans.

> My thoughts about teaching have been given a jolt this year . . . I was introduced to something which stopped and beguiled me, muddling my sense of purpose, and I am thankful for it. . . . We learn by using what we know as a basis for further knowledge, applying our own individual techniques to progress from the known to the unknown.

> I suppose my whole attitude about curriculum has changed because I no longer know what it is. Curriculum implies an organized attempt to teach something. Learning as I now understand it does not happen in an organized way. . . . My attempts in the future will be based in my own understanding of the universe, or small portions of it . . .

> Before I had lamented that science could not be more fun and more experientially oriented, but I thought that was just naive, moreover 'too artistic.' Now I believe that scientific learning is tremendously experiential and scientific thinking, particularly my own in an experiential framework, is fascinating to me.

> I think literature and art were always presented to me as realms that I determined . . . [This work suggests] that the physical world is just as legitimately processed through our individuality as the arts and can therefore become as much a part of us, can feed some growing source within ourselves. This is revolutionary to me.

> A mind that has no questions, no curiosity about a subject, cannot fully comprehend and assimilate answers handed out by a teacher. That is not to say a student can't memorize facts and answers and spit them back out on a test. I am sure that at some time in my education I learned about mirrors, angles of reflection (or is it refraction?), and so on, but because I had no practical use for the knowledge, and had no curiosity about the subject, once I had passed my test, I promptly forgot just about everything. . . .

When I worked with mirrors [I] asked myself questions others may have found simplistic, but that I really wanted to know the answer to.

Even if one knows a great deal about something already, there is always still something new to learn about it especially if he doesn't let existing notions and biases get in the way of incorporating new ideas. Adults often think that knowledge is expert book knowledge, and that there are only certain ways they are supposed to look at things.

Confusion was a term we were made to feel comfortable about. I remember times during my years of schooling when I preferred to live with my uncertainty than to make it known. [Here] confusion was considered the first step towards understanding.

I studied optics for half a year in college with labs and manuals, and I venture to say that my work with a mirror and a wall (two familiar items that don't scare me a bit) involved me more than all the rest. I [now] understand something I was [already] supposed to know. . . .

Although I, my students, and my curriculum have undergone change as a result of my learning, something else has happened which has affected me personally. I am more courageous. I try to understand things that I would not have contemplated before. This is perhaps the most important learning that I have made. If I want to solve a problem all I have to do is start thinking.

This sense of discovery about focusing on subject matter infused itself into every aspect of my life. My friends enjoyed the things I was seeing and wondering about: the green and pink shiny parts on pigeons: was the green greener because it reflected the grass? We'd have to look at the pigeons on concrete. Questions were coming, . . . a rush of finding a questions.

When I go back to teaching, I will make a conscious effort to allow my students the same respect for their ideas and thoughts that I have been allowed in this course. I never before realized how much the freedom to be 'wrong' without being embarrassed meant. If it is that important to an adult, think how necessary it must be to [a child].

I always had a certain myopia for everything to do with science; and if I analyze my attitude a bit it seems to me that I maintained this lack of curiosity with a certain pride.

    For me . . . whether the moon was waxing or waning left me totally indifferent. I could spend a marvelous summer evening contemplating the moon in the heavens, seduced by its beauty, but I never would have asked myself why or how. This lack of interest is surely due to a certain incapacity, carefully maintained throughout my studies, and above all I think by the irritation my colleagues caused me with their 'scientific discoveries' which I found infantile. . . .

I am not yet over it, but every Friday now I have the impression that we . . . are going to discover something marvellous. . . . What astonishes me above all is this capacity to push things always further.

At school I am making marvellous discoveries. My pupils who never were interested in school and who never brought in anything for the class give me with great generosity any material that I need for the experiments. They impatiently await Saturday morning [a school day in Geneva] to do the experiments. Sometimes they interrupt their work to experiment. They plant seeds in every pot.

What has surprised me the most is that since we have been working together in science they listen to 'scientific' radio programs for children; they pick up litle puzzles, and stick me with them. So I am listening now, too, so I can answer them! And in September they only listened to the pop singers!

Together, I have the impression that we are gaining a 'third dimension.' Our spirit is getting more curious.

I also think that during our moments of 'science' work, their attitude has changed: they communicate with me differently, a little as equal to equal. The girls, after some hesitation, are very interested, and their relationships with the boys are better.

Personally, I am overwhelemd by their ways of tackling a problem (I have the impression that I know them better through this work), by their imagination, and by the solutions they come up with.

Now, I would like to continue this experience with them, to discover and practice alone, and above all to read introductory science books.

I don't know if I am on the right track, but in the evening when I go out I look at the sky to see if I see the moon.

Teachers' Work With Children

What I look for in the teachers' accounts of their work with children is evidence that they are at ease watching and talking to the children about material phenomena; that they are not feeling that they must keep control over what the children do and learn.

Snow.   Here is an example of a report from a kindergarten teacher.

In December, some children brought in snow and pieces of ice. They put them in a big aluminum tub, that was soon about 3/4 full. Two or three children observed that it melted, and there was water.

After Christmas vacation, they noticed that the water in the tub had disappeared. ''In its place'' [as the children put it] there were pieces of grass, little pebbles, pieces of wood, earth, etc.

There were various remarks, like the following:

- "The teacher poured it out."
- "The water ran out a little hole."
- "Somebody drank it."
- ["And where do all these things come from?"]
- "Somebody thought it was the wastebasket."
- "The janitor put stuff in it."

All these remarks led us to do it again. We waited for snow. As soon as it came, each child went and filled a plastic cup and put a nametag on it. Then they tried to say ahead of time what would happen. [In general they said either that they did not know, or that the snow would turn into water. When they looked a few hours later, here is how the teacher reported what they said and saw]:

In some cups, a mixture of water and unmelted snow; lots of dirt ("Snow is dirty!" "You shouldn't eat it!"); "My nametag's still there"; "My water's red" (in fact, his nametag fell in the water, and since it was red cardboard, the color came out of it); many comments on how much or little water there was in a cup. (Sermet & Sermet, 1978, p. 7)

There was no concluding remark on this weekly write-up, but one comment on the final report was, "What a relief not to judge or to be judged!"

Water and Air.   The next example provides an occasion to discuss a number of principles for helping children explore. Just as with teachers, the challenge is to keep them engaged, with ever more ideas of things to do.

A good question or suggestion is one that allows children to create their own ways to proceed. An indicator of a good question or suggestion is that the teacher does not have to be heard from again—the children are full of ideas of things to do. I think it is worth mentioning that a teacher's "why does that happen?" question rarely has that quality. Usually, answers to such questions are stereotyped, contradict one another, and do not lead anywhere. Questions that keep children engaged are, rather, questions like the following: What do you have to do to get that to happen again? Try to make it (rounder, slower, higher, lighter, quicker, etc.). Can you find any more like that? What did you do that was different from what she did? Could you manage to . . . ? Could you make a drawing to show the others what you found? Try doing the same thing with this instead. How is it different now from what it was before?

The following example is drawn, not from a classroom, but from weekly "practice" sessions by student teachers. Two of them worked with groups of four 9-year-olds. They based their work on some activities we had done together in class (they were, in fact, from the group who had explored siphons), and presented the children with basins of water, glass jars, cups, escargot shells, eye droppers, syringes, tubes, and balloons. They invited the children to work in any way they wished with these materials.

In one session, children were filling and emptying syringes. There always seemed to be one bothersome air bubble. They asked the children whether they could get rid of it. This led the children to try putting the syringe in all possible positions, until they found that they had to point it upwards, "because the bubble 'floats' on the water in the syringe, and when they push the water up, the air goes first" (Kuster & Rielle, 1975, p. 3).

In another session, Daniel was playing with an eye dropper.

> The plastic bulb intrigues him. He doesn't know what he did, but the plastic is stuck flat . . . and he'd like to get it unstuck. He doesn't notice that his finger is blocking the other end of the dropper, so intent is he on the bulb itself. When he takes his finger off the end, the bulb takes its round form . . . I ask him if he could make it stick again. [She might have asked him why he thought it was stuck!] He hesitates. He says he doesn't know. I suggest that he try to make it happen again. After two or three tries he comes to show me that first you have to squeeze the bulb and then block the other end. . . . To "unstick" it all you have to do is take your finger off. (Kuster & Rielle, p. 5)

Even so, these student teachers worked hard at finding ways to keep the children engaged in their activities. On one of their weekly reports, they wrote, "We know what you are going to say—There are too many 'why's." They asked, for example, "Why do the bubbles rise?" and "Why doesn't the cork stay on the bottom?". Neither of these questions led anywhere. By contrast, in a later session, they appreciated the insights of a child who had a cork stuck at the bottom of a narrow tube. What he did was to fill the tube with water—and the cork floated to the top—a greater manifestation of familiarity with the physical world than any answer to those "why" questions would have been.

Musical Instruments.   A music teacher who took this course incorporated the same approach into her work with a class of 10 behaviorally difficult children between the ages of 8 and 11. They explored ways to make musical instruments.

The exploration started with finding many ways to make different sounds with their own hands—clap them flat, clap them on the sides, clap them with the fingers spread out, clap with the fingers of one hand in the palm of the other; rub them together; make a fist with one and hit it with the other; scratch one hand with the other; hit one hand with one finger of the other.

They used these variations in hitting other objects—wooden tables, formica tables, windows, the sink, the floor—and then tried different things as drum sticks on these objects: flat sticks, slender sticks, bamboo sticks and chop sticks, sticks with erasers stuck onto the ends, and sticks with balls of wool fixed onto the ends. They struck the sounding objects with movements that were supple or rigid, energetic or timid, using the whole arm, or using only a slight hand motion.

They explored their own breathing—deep and slow, fast and jerky— and tried changing the shapes of their lips. Then they tried different ways of blowing into tubes—cardboard, plastic, and bamboo, open and closed. Pitch became a factor of interest now, because it was different in different tubes. Given that it varies with the length of the tube, the diameter of the tube, the degree of pressure of the lips, and the force of the movement of the air, the whole domain remained, as the teacher said, ''rather mysterious'' (Piuz, 1978, p. 5). Some children were able to do some sorting out of these factors, even during this beginning. Francis, for example, blew by turns into each end of a piece of bamboo with a knot closer to one end than to the other, and did not understand why the two ends produced different pitches. This question stayed with him as he blew into other pieces of bamboo, and he discovered that the longer they were the deeper they were.

Pitch produced by plucking strings is complicated, also: it depends on the length of the string, the material it is made of, its thickness, and the tension it is under. The children had partial insights into these factors, in the early explorations. Gabrielle, for example, sorted out the influence of the length of the string: when she pushed the string down to the board and plucked one end of it, the sound went higher. She moved her finger to many different places, listening for the pitch each time. When the children started making instruments, the first stringed instruments they built had a very gentle sound, being simply strung across flat boards. Drawing on their hitting activities, the children started placing these instrument boards onto other objects, like the tables they had earlier explored. Gabrielle went one better. She had replaced her finger with a half coconut shell, which she could slide up and down easily under the string, for a change in pitch. Her exploratory mode then took her to turn the coconut the other side up—and now it served, in addition, as a sounding board.

The construction of small flutes—bamboo pipes with finger holes— was the most instructive to the teacher.

The construction is delicate, and requires a lot of precision . . . I tried to explain the importance of the position of the knot [in the bamboo], the necessity of measuring the positions of the holes, etc., etc. To no avail; these explanations did not interest them at all. . . . They all leapt in. . . .

Seeing how busy and enthusiastic they were, I let everything go, wondering what was going to turn out. . . . In fact, there was no shortage of mishaps. [And yet they each produced some whistle, pipe or flute with which they were pleased.]

This construction shows how hard it is to reconcile what the teacher knows with what the child knows . . . My first wish was to put the pupils through the same route [as I had taken]. By their detour, I think they were able to understand . . . better. (Piuz, 1978, p. 33)

Shadows. The kindergarten teacher in this example felt constrained by her inspector always to work with the whole class at a time. She nonetheless engaged the children in a study of shadows. (The room was very dark and was lit essentially by three overhead lights.)

First the children looked for shadows in the room, and traced around their contours. Many objects in the room did not have clear shadows, given the three overlapping light sources, so to begin associating shadows with objects they chose a large drum, whose shadow was large and clear. To their surprise, when they moved the drum to the center of their circle, its clear shadow was no longer clear; it had a fuzzy, triple shadow. They turned off all the lights, then one or two at a time, and exclaimed with great astonishment, first, that the lights seemed responsible for the shadows, and then, that switching on and off different lights made the shadow move.

When the children used a flashlight, they were enchanted to see that moving the light made the object itself seem to move. They moved the shadows around in all directions. "The shadow's huge!" "You can't see it very well at the end." "It's skinny!" "Now the shadow's real little, and you can see it really good." Shining the lamp directly from above onto a pot, they talked of the shadow "sliding under the pot."

On another day, the teacher asked them how they could make a shadow on the blackboard.

"We have to turn on all the lights." They did.

"We have to have something." They went to get a teddy bear, and one child placed it against the blackboard.

"You can't see anything, you can't see any shadow."

"I know!" one child exclaimed, seizing the teddy bear and moving it slightly away from the blackboard. A small, pale shadow was visible.

"Yeah, but you can't see what it is," another child said.

What to do? She let them think about it. After a moment, Giorgio said, "We need a whole lot of light." She gave them a flashlight, and let them figure it out. They had a hard time getting themselves

organized . . . the flashlight was too close to the teddy bear . . . the
teddy bear was too close to the blackboard, and so on. Finally they
succeeded.

"You can see the shadow, you can see the shadow!" "It's funny, you
can see the ears." "But you can't see its face."

What to do?

"I know, you have to turn it around!" The child who was holding
the bear turned it 180 degrees, so the shadow didn't change. Stephane
grabbed it and turned it sideways. Everyone could see the shape of the
nose!

Now the children wanted to look at the shadows of their own bodies
against this blackboard. One after another they paraded in front of the
blackboard, and immobilized themselves before the rays of the flashlight. "You can't see your shadow, Nicholas, get out of the way!" But
when he got out of the way, there was of course no shadow! There was
also the problem of profiles. The children wanted to see each other in
profile. But each child wanted to see his own shadow on the board, so
he stayed with his back to the light source.

After they had more or less worked out these problems, Alain
brought up a paper man he had just cut out. Its shadow was a great
success, and each one wanted to make a shadow object. That became
the activity of another day.

The children first drew their shadow objects with no regard for the
importance of the profile. They drew mouths, noses, pockets, buttons,
doors, and so forth. When they projected their shadows, they were
often quite unrecognizable. The teacher let them think about that, and
one child finally announced that she was going to make holes for the
eyes and mouth of her figure. This idea caught on, of course, although
the realization of the desired outlines was not easily accomplished.

The next problem that the children had to face was that they
themselves, their hands and arms, interfered with the shadows of their
objects. Left to think about that problem they added sticks.

As the children displayed the shadows of the objects they had made,
they spontaneously started moving them, and one of them started to
tell a story. The teacher took a cue from that, and set up the slide
projector and a real screen. The children were so absorbed by working
their marionettes that they lost their habitual timidity, and their stories
were better than ever. The children in the audience listened better than
ever, also.

The last class activity involved the shadows of the children's own
bodies again, this time with the projector and screen. One child at a
time stood in the beam of light, behind the other children, who were
looking at the screen where her shadow was. The children did

characteristic gestures or actions, much to the amusement of their peers, and then they started miming activities. They got better and better, both at the miming and at showing the essence of the action in the shadow (adapted from Bernasconi, 1975).

That was the grand finale of the class study of shadows, although the children kept looking for, finding, and commenting on shadows in the classroom for the rest of the year. For some of the activities in this account, one might wish that the children had been working on their own, in small groups, and at various times of the day. However, it seems to me that this work with the entire class at once had some advantages, also. A shared enterprise in a group becomes bigger than itself, each person building not only on the ideas, but on the eagerness of all of the others. I think some of this effect can be seen even in this story of 5-year-olds.

CURRICULUM AND EVALUATION

So far, I have talked only about teacher education and what individual teachers can do. I would like to close by talking briefly about two kinds of support teachers need, even if they do believe that children construct their own knowledge, on the basis of becoming engaged in the fascinations of the world, and even if they are willing to follow children's explorations.

Curriculum

In many school systems, science is not an important part of the elementary curriculum. This can work as an advantage or as a disadvantage. Above all, it means that nobody is likely to care very much what teachers do in science. If teachers are full of ideas of their own, this can give them freedom to work with their own ideas; nobody will be upset that they are not doing what they are supposed to do. On the other hand, of course, it means that nobody will be upset if they do nothing at all; or it means that if they want to do something in science, and do not feel capable of going it alone, nobody is likely to give them much help.

In school systems where attention is given to science, the flip sides of these advantages and disadvantages appear. On the one hand some help may be available. On the other hand, teachers are not likely to have a choice about what science to teach, and there is likely to be quite restrictive evaluation. At the end of this chapter I discuss evaluation briefly. First, I discuss some ideas about curriculum.

It does make sense to me that a school system that includes science in its elementary curriculum should be concerned that the children encounter a range of phenomena—plants, animals, the solar system, heat, light and shadows, water and air, balances, flashlights, bicycles—and that curriculum committees try to plan accordingly. It does not make sense to me, for reasons I mentioned at the beginning of this chapter, that children should be expected to state some form of authoritative knowledge about all of these things, but rather that they have a familiarity with them, be intrigued by them, and feel that finding out more about them is within their capabilities.

A curriculum committee, then, might start by placing topics like these at various grade levels. But then the hard work is to offer teachers ways of getting into the topics. Textbooks, I submit, do not help, based as they are on the idea of presenting carefully ordered pieces of somebody else's knowledge. Assuming that teacher education goes hand in hand with the introduction of curriculum, and that teachers are prepared to concentrate their efforts on helping the children develop their own knowledge, rather than trying to impose on them someone else's knowledge, what is needed is a repertory of interesting phenomena for children to explore, suggestions of ways for teachers to engage children, activities and questions that have intrigued other children. Henriques' work contributes in this way. A number of my students have also tried to do this.

Gears. Two teachers (who had worked both with me and with Henriques) were granted leave from their own classrooms and worked in the classrooms of other teachers who had also taken this course. They set out to study gears, and a large part of their contribution was the elaboration of inexpensive, accessible materials, made essentially of corrugated cardboard. Pressboard wheels of different sizes had dowel axles. Corrugated cardboard strips were glued around the periphery. The dowels then could be stuck into sheets of styrofoam so the gear wheels would be engaged. Long thin strips of corrugated cardboard served as belts to connect other gear wheels that did not contact each other directly. Additional materials included various round objects, extra corrugated cardboard, elastic, string, plastic gear wheels, tubes, and small objects to serve as weights.

Six- and 7-year-olds used the materials to make vehicles and windmills whose wheels would turn. They essentially ignored the belts, string, and styrofoam supports. Eight- and 9-year-olds assembled complicated gear arrangements in which every wheel turned with the pull of a single string. They tried building construction cranes and ski-lifts. Eleven- and 12-year-olds made similar constructions, also exploring the directions that the wheels turned, and how many times one wheel turned compared with another. Their questions eventually took them into investigations of bicycles and clocks.

The published teachers' guide includes photos of the children's work, as well as the children's own drawings, and excerpts from their questions and conversations (Baeryswil & Larpin, 1979).

Pulse Beats. Another teacher worked in her own class, developing ways of engaging her students in a study of the circulatory system, a required part of her science curriculum. She decided to start from explorations of their own pulse beats.

> Initially I was doubtful about how far we could go with our investigation. Part of my reticence was my own belief that it would be difficult to find out much about the circulatory system without the aid of books, charts, pickled hearts and the inimitable lecture about arteries and veins. . . . I was very pleasantly surprised and amazed to discover how much investigation was generated from the pulse work. (Young, 1986, p.2)

A science teacher already, at first she found herself focussing on large, unanswerable questions, of which "why" was one example.

> My first two sessions were different from subsequent ones because I was new at this method . . . In both sessions I initiated a great many of the ideas; we spent little time on each of them. . . . They were happy to stick with readable messurements. I, though, was bent on getting to some immediate "why's" and ended up muddling them and stifling their efforts.
>
> I asked point blank why they had a pulse which exhibited itself the way it does. In retrospect I am astounded that I did this, but at the time I had this inner feeling of desperation to keep "things moving" . . . . I asked if the blood is continuous through every tube or are there gaps where there is no blood. Wally said gaps and Matt said continuous. . . . I have no idea how a few minutes of work with pulse was supposed to equip them with information which would allow them to answer. . . . Other than actually taking our pulse in a few places, we barely broached other observations which would have been necessary before venturing to see relationships and possibilities. (Young, 1986, p.7)

In subsequent sessions she found "the students were delighted sticking to the 'what's' of pulse-taking" (Young, 1986, p.10), and they ended up coming, themselves, to some of the "why's"—which then they attached to their own means of finding out.

Taking pulse beats in different ways, at different places, in different circumstances is an accessible way to approach circulation—accessible both for teachers and for students. Young's report includes what the children did, what they said about what they did, what they found interesting and what they found dull, the questions they themselves introduced and pursued. It also includes, and this is a great part of its value, the teacher's own comments, as exemplified in the quotes just given, about what she thought about what she did, which of her initiatives she thought worked well, and which she thought were mistaken, and why. This work has not been published but it is the sort of contribution which I see as expanding teachers' repertories of ways to engage children in explorations and to build on their knowledge.

Trees.   Yet another way to go about developing curriculum suggestions that expand teachers' repertories and thus enable them to work productively with children in areas they might not have chosen to teach is to work with a small group of children, paying close attention to what engages them and causes them to give thought to the subject, and what those thoughts are. Julyan, a teacher and biologist, looked for ways to engage 11-year-olds in studying trees. Just as Young's pulse work was developed as a way to approach "circulation," so Julyan's work was developed as a way to approach "photosynthesis," although in both cases, the phenomena—pulse beats or trees—were introduced as themselves, without reference to any particular idea they were meant to illuminate. In both cases, the criterion was to make these subject matters—these parts of the world—accessible and interesting to children.

Like Young, Julyan found that the students became interested in particularities, not the general questions she had first had in mind.

> For example, I had thought that I would watch the boys develop a theory about trees. Instead their work revealed an interest in . . . individual trees. . . . Our initial conversation about nutrients and roots led me to believe that the boys understood more than they actually did. I had thought that our work could lead to a deeper understanding of nutrients and the relationship between nutrients and what they see on the tree. When we began to look at the tree itself, it became clear to me that our exploration would center first on what we saw. . . . By gathering data, . . . [the boys] began to develop a curiosity about trees and how they work. . . . I believe that the curiosity grew out of the opportunity to explore something of interest at their own pace and without adult "explanations." My data about their understanding of trees has rein-

forced my belief that there is an enormous difference between students using the correct words and having a complete understanding . . . [This work] reveals some of the mystery and complexity of learning. (Julyan, 1986a, p.3)

Here are some of the particular observations and questions that got them interested. The boys referred to the trees they were watching with different, descriptive names—the fuzzy-bud tree (magnolia), the many-buds tree (maple), the ball tree (dogwood), the yellow bush (forsythia), and the snake tree (with catkins).

"Wow, this looks good! All the little buds have turned into flowers, not leaves! . . . Oh, look, there's one opening up. These are nice. Maybe this one will be just flowers . . . And the ones up there are all open because they get more sun." [Oh, the sun makes them open?] "Because it gives them more energy. See, these down here, it's not open a bit." [So they don't get very much sun?] . . . "The sun's shining on them but there's a shadow on the other side." (Julyan, 1986a, p.11)

Another tree, another day, provoked the following observations. Different children take part in this discussion.

"Oh this is wierd, it's turning more green now . . . We thought that this branch here would turn more yellow. But it turned more green . . . All the flowers are dropping off. Maybe it means that all the flowers are dropping off, the leaves are coming in . . . Maybe it's done flowering . . . I thought that the green would turn to flowers." . . . "I never knew that these trees were first yellow and then green." "Yeah. I thought they were green and then yellow." "Yeah, most of them do that." "Yeah, that's a new idea because most of them have leaves and flowers, at least, that's the way I thought it." . . . "First leaves, then flowers." "And now this one has flowers and then leaves." [Did any of the others have first flowers, then leaves?] . . . "I think that one over there." . . . [Yeah, that one had flowers then leaves. What about the fuzzy bud tree?] "That doesn't have leaves yet, just flowers." (Tone of voice implies that because it doesn't have leaves yet, it can't be counted in this category! Wish I had noted that sooner.) . . . "It had buds, then leaves. No, buds then flowers, buds then flowers." (Julyan, 1986b, pp. 3–4)

On another day, concern for a particular tree led to this close observation and careful thinking:

During our check of the fuzzy-bud tree, we noticed some buds beneath the tree. Dan became concerned when he realized how many buds were on the ground.

"Somebody knocked off all of these. [Do you think they've been knocked off or fallen off? Can you see where they might be coming from?] Maybe it came from here." (He then finds the branch that we had marked and counted the buds on last time—13 buds.) "1,2,3,4,5,6,7." (He picks up a bud on the ground.) "It looks dead." [What makes it look dead?] "It's brown. It's not too healthy. Maybe it's dead and that's why it's falling off, because it got too cold."

As we moved on to the many-buds tree, the problem of the fuzzy-bud tree was clearly on his mind, as seen by our conversation between trees. [Do you have any ideas about how trees work yet?] "Not really, they sort of get fed by the ground and the sun and—. Let's go back and look at the other tree like the one that's dying and see if they're on the ground there. If they're not on the ground over there then maybe there's something wrong with the first tree."

We did, and Dan discovered that the fuzzy-bud tree on the opposite side of the street had no buds on the ground, only the shells of buds. (Julyan, 1986a, p. 7)

On his way home, Dan checked yet another fuzzy-bud tree, and reported that it did not have buds on the ground under it. He concluded that the tree he was concerned about was indeed sick.

This study has a broader scope than Young's, because Julyan had opportunity to work with children over a longer period. Children watched trees in the fall, when the leaves were changing color, as well as in the spring, and the areas that came into the study included water, seeds, the function of green leaves, and the relationships of the motions of the sun and the moon to the changing seasons. If we consider curriculum to be, as I have suggested elsewhere, ways of engaging students in giving thought to those matters that we think important (Duckworth, 1986), then such accounts are a form of curriculum: accounts of what teachers did, how children responded, what captured children's interest, what they thought, what they did about what they thought, and—of central importance to other teachers—the teachers' thoughts about what they themselves did, the problems as well as the triumphs.

Evaluation

Clearly, the kind of teaching I am calling for is difficult to assess through multiple choice tests. If elementary school science is to be evaluated in that way, the battle is lost. Multiple-choice tests are not the only possibility for evaluation, however. Educational Testing Services's Edward Chittenden has piloted a different kind of evaluation, one that shares a lot of assumptions with the kind of teaching we have been describing. He has started to develop standardized evaluation procedures which are not multiple choice. In introducing this work, Chittenden (1984) said the following:

The limitations of the multiple choice format for assessing pupil knowledge and higher level skills have long been recognized by both test producers and consumers, but practical matters surrounding test administration and scoring have meant that the format remains the dominant one in achievement testing, . . . With respect to science testing the limitations are three-fold:

- The selected-response mode masks the nature of pupils' . . . [own] knowledge and understanding. Children not only answer someone else's questions but they must also choose among someone else's answers.
- It is extremely difficult . . . to use multiple choice exercises for assessing productive thinking and problem solving.
- An exclusive emphasis upon "best" and "correct" answers is antithetical to goals of science education and sets a poor model for educational assessment. (p. 14)

Chittenden recommended that "the inclusion of free-response exercises or items should be a required feature of a testing program in science" (Chittenden, 1984, p. 14), and his pilot study indicates ways that such items could be developed, administered, and scored. They turn out to be interesting to both teachers and children, as well as to be compatible with the kind of curriculum I have been discussing.

The topics covered in this pilot work are those that are given emphasis in the New York City program. Here is one example of such a question. "Some weeds are growing in the cracks of a new sidewalk. Can you think of some ways the weeds got there?" Chittenden reported:

teachers noted that less than half of the children explicitly implicated seed dispersal in explaining how "weeds got there" despite the fact that seeds and their travels constitute a prominent topic in primary science. Upon subsequent questioning, many children appear to believe that weeds sprout spontaneously from the earth; they are not classified as "real" plants. "Weeds grow by themselves"; "They just need sun and water"; "You plant flower seeds and get weeds." (Chittenden, 1984, p. 24)

Another question was, "What is the sun made of?" and answers ranged from "one large atom" to "billions of stars joined together," passing through "fire and electricity from the earth" (Chittenden, 1984, p. 18).

Answers to "What kinds of living things might you find in the playground?" included bacteria, birds, and swing sets (Chittenden, 1984, p. 19).

Chittenden proposed, as a purpose for testing in elementary science, "to elucidate the nature of students' thinking—their understandings, misconceptions, and prior knowledge." He pointed out that, in this case:

> the tone of the questioning must invite their participation. Teachers noted that children were sensitive to the difference between questions that asked for their thinking, and questions that asked, in effect, whether they know the "correct" answer . . . One teacher reported that a number of children said they liked the open-ended test although it was lengthy and posed difficult questions. When asked why they liked it, they responded, "Because you wanted to find out what we thought." (Chittenden, 1984, pp. 18–19)

This kind of testing returns us to the three obstacles mentioned at the outset of this chapter. Most immediately, it reassures us with the thought that evaluation procedures need not be stifling. Second, it acknowledges the teacher as an intelligent professional, putting her in the position of responding to the children's knowledge, and deciding what to do next. Finally, coming full circle, it brings into relief the assumption that it is the *learner*'s knowledge with which we are concerned.

ACKNOWLEDGMENT

The writer is grateful to Brenda Engel for a critical reading at a critical moment.

REFERENCES

Baeryswil, E., & Larpin, D. (1979). *Les Engrenages*. Lausanne, Guilde de Documentation de la SPR.

Bernasconi, M.-C. (1975). *Experience sur l'ombre*. Unpublished manuscript, University of Geneva.

Brooks, J. (1986). Unpublished manuscript, Harvard University, Cambridge, MA.

Chittenden, E. (1984). *Interim report: Committee for Assessment in Science Education*. Princeton, NJ: Educational Testing Service.

Duckworth, E. (1986). Teaching as research. *Harvard Educational Review, 56*(4), 481–495.

Evans, C. (1986). [Unpublished remarks presented at Second Rainbow Conference on Science Education, New York].

Hawkins, D. (1978). Critical barriers to science learning, *Outlook, 29*, 3–23.

Julyan, C. (1986a). *Trees.* Unpublished manuscript, Harvard University, Cambridge, MA.

Julyan, C. (1986). Unpublished field report, Harvard University, Cambridge, MA.

Kuster, L., Rielle, L. (1975). Unpublished field reports, University of Geneva.

Piuz, G. (1978). *Des Sons, Une Voie.* Unpublished manuscript, University of Geneva.

Schwartz, E. (1986). *An over-repeating story.* In C. Traugh, R. Kanevsky, A. Martin, A. Seletsky, K. Woolf, & L. Strieb (1986). *Speaking out: Teachers on teaching,* (pp. 22–27). Grand Forks, ND: North Dakota Study Group on Evaluation.

Sermet, G., & Sermet, L. (1978). Unpublished manuscript, University of Geneva.

Young, L. (1986). *Teacher as learner in research and the classroom.* Unpublished manuscript, Harvard University, Cambridge, MA.

3

Stressing Dialogic Skill

Jack Easley
University of Illinois at Urbana-Champaign

PROBLEMS OF AUTHORITARIAN SCIENCE IN AMERICAN ELEMENTARY SCHOOLS

Elementary school science teaching in the United States is a critical area of the curriculum in need of repair, because so many teachers are anxious about science and quite unintentionally transfer their anxiety to their pupils either by science avoidance or by authoritarian presentations of science terminology and generalizations. The same attitudes are also reflected in other institutions of society like those of secondary and higher education, the media, and government. People often feel afraid to reveal that they never did understand the physics, chemistry, physiology, or astronomy they have been exposed to. These subjects, besides a tendency to involve mathematics in unfamiliar forms and contexts, may be especially frightening because they are prone to surprising departures from ordinary meanings of words and are also prone to frustrating rigidity in allowed meanings.

Science anxiety has its exceptions. Elementary school teachers can have meaningful daily encounters out of school with meteorology, horticulture, and botany (e.g., TV weather maps make sufficient connection with the elementary school curriculum that teachers can feel comfortable with them). Plant morphology and physiology can be studied to illuminate a person's experience of house and garden plants, resulting in a lot of questions being raised, experiences being shared,

61

and technical information being accumulated. Neither field is likely to involve teachers in basic questions of life, matter, and energy that make other sciences the more troublesome.

Elementary school teachers often unconsciously imitate the authoritarian approach of scientists, when they teach, and of specialized science teachers, who try to overcome the conceptual confusion of most of their students by leaning on their authority, striving to give error-free lectures and exacting examinations. Elementary school teachers often uncritically fall into the trap of viewing scientists as infallible authorities whose pronouncements cannot be understood by the vast majority of people and thus can only be memorized. Many secondary and college-level science teachers fall into the same trap, and research data (e.g., Driver, Guesne, & Tiberghien, 1985; West & Pines, 1985) indicate that error-generating preconceptions usually persist through several years of high school or college-level instruction. A few professional in-service teacher-education programs, and this book, do promote science understandings (Duckworth, 1983, 1987. Cf. Henriques' analysis of teacher responses, pp. 179ff.).

Scientists, themselves, perhaps because they have been skeptics from childhood, often enjoy disagreeing with each other and arguing many controversial points, but they do this outside of the classroom. In class, because of the pressure of covering their courses' parts of a vast knowledge base, they rarely provide students the opportunities to hear conflicting views.

In spite of the authoritarian way most scientists teach, they are likely to be more impressed with those students in their classes who can articulate critical thought, and who thus contribute to the correcting of errors in their struggle to understand, than those students who study passively and uncritically. Private efforts to rationalize a point in text, lecture, or lab are likely to be rewarded with new metaphors and continued efforts to explain the confusing concepts.

Science-specialist teachers typically seem to pitch the level of complexity in class so that about half the students can follow well, or pretty well, and about half feel lost, with half of the latter so lost they eventually drop the course perhaps to try again later. The dropouts, or those who make low grades in spite of hard work, include many critical thinkers who can detect gaps in scientific reasoning but who lack the verbal ability to communicate them to inflexible teachers.

Those few students who persist autonomously in dealing with science critically and creatively, in spite of the authoritarian teaching they regularly encounter, may have had encouragement from parents or from an unusual teacher. It seems to me very likely they also developed confidence from personal out-of-school experiences, in effect, becoming "amateur scientists," who tried out and thus tested their grasp of most of the science terms, procedures, or principles they may have heard. Elementary teachers, with few experiences of this sort in childhood, tended to memorize uncritically what they interpreted their teachers to be saying, so as to repeat it on demand. They are often surprised to learn, however, that some of what they remembered was considered inadequate or even wrong. When they teach, they tend to take on an authoritative stance as a defense against the children who might challenge them if given an opportunity to do so.

Because of the complexities children can get into, I see only two distinct ways in which most teachers or future teachers could improve their science teaching: Either they would have to become gradually, but seriously, amateur scientists themselves or they would have to become sensitive listeners who support and assist children in their often frustrating struggle with their own ideas. Teachers in this second approach take pride that their pupils are discovering that they have and use ideas and are also discovering some of the limitations of their ideas. (Cf. chapter 5, pp. 171–178).

The first approach could begin by teachers critically studying and experimenting with phenomena in which they already have an interest and some confidence. These teachers might grow plants to study their developing morphology and soil biochemistry or collect weather maps and make local predictions, and, for comparison record the weather. It is not difficult to recognize such lovers of doing practical science. They appear to be few in number.

The second approach is far more likely, it seems to me, but also is more beneficial to children. Teachers can improve their science teaching by concentrating their attention mainly on promoting pupils' creative and critical thinking about their environment and sensitively studying ways to promote that kind of thinking in all the children in their classrooms. Nearly all teachers I know love children enough for me to believe they would greatly enjoy "teaching by listening" (Easley & Zwoyer, 1975, cf. chapter 5, p. 179).

Some teachers using peer-group dialogues and open-ended tasks in their science classes were influenced in a course or workshop I led, where they saw videotapes that Elizabeth Easley and I brought back from Japan of elementary school mathematics and science lessons taught in this way. Still, it was not a simple thing for most of them to learn to stand aside when the children in their classes were discussing science. (Making that change with math story problems was easier than with computation, and it was easier with science experiments than with health lessons.) This method conflicts with teachers' usual understanding of what their job is. Working out such conflicts satisfactorily takes time and supportive encouragement.

Many of the teachers' concerns were not so forthcoming as the children's concerns about conceptual conflicts in science lessons. It took me some years just to begin to understand the issue of teachers' authority in their terms. It was difficult for me to feel how nervous they felt when not guiding their pupils' thoughts toward the official responses. To be sure, there was evidence of that, and there was also evidence of nervousness about not understanding the official textbook explanations of scientific phenomena themselves. But whom do you ask if you have questions? If, when you were a student, your teachers did not seem to understand or want to answer your questions, you may have felt nervous about your ability to ask "an intelligent question." So, when you are a teacher you lean on the text as the authority selected for your class by the local school authorities.

However, before most of their pupils will openly say what they think, it may be necessary for many teachers to admit to themselves that they are not adequate authorities for the content their class is studying, and to stop playing that role. That is understandably difficult for teachers who have been trying to rationalize their performance as a content expert for years. Finding a new role, by watching videotaped model classes, can help.

Teaching seventh-grade general science was very difficult for me until I realized that children saw science as controversial. Then I could react with interest to the different concepts they exhibited instead of trying to correct them myself. On the other hand, elementary school teachers who are not science enthusiasts often know from experience that their own deeply rooted science anxiety handicaps them when they encounter conceptually conflicting material. Such teachers may take a great deal of pride in creating a supportive atmosphere in which children can build confidence in doing their own science reasoning on difficult tasks. Fear of public humiliation about science when students are wrong seems to become progressively debilitating for most children and their teachers, but science anxiety is something the young largely lack before they enter elementary school.

I can recall as an undergraduate thinking that only physics, music, and mathematics counted as knowledge. I could not see the point of studying anything else, because controversies could so easily undermine whatever it was the professors said. When I became a physics teacher, my attitude was the same, and I was dismayed that so few of my students were interested and that so many of them seemed lost. I am sure that I regularly put them down for getting things "wrong." But I also recall that I could not stand criticism myself.

Here lies the chief problem of science education: Contrary to popular belief, firm belief in one's knowledge is a dangerous thing for what it can do to discourage others and oneself from learning. The more difficult problem about it is that one pretends to speak for the scientific establishment, whose best authorities are likely to be quite sensitive to the lack of proper qualifying conditions, if not downright errors, in what you have said (see pp. 89–91).

In my experience, more challenging tasks can motivate more children and can help them develop their confidence, especially if they are supported by their teachers. What is puzzling to many teachers and future teachers, however, is that students working on such problems often disagree with their peers and are not able to resolve problems, and yet they are not discouraged. It is as though children, like scientists, know that they are better off if they can work out ideas themselves than if they are given the most authoritative answer they do not understand.

There is a difficulty for many teachers in this approach. What role does the scientific knowledge they have play in their teaching if they must hold back from giving it to children? To answer that problem, and to promote dialogue among their students, they often adopt an extremely relativistic position, and say to children and to their colleagues, "In science, there are no right or wrong answers." I would prefer they say that they are not in a good position to decide what is right and what is wrong, but reward their students for the steps that have been made in responsible thinking.

Teachers who dare to pose questions about physics, even though they know little about it formally, can however, run very successful physics lessons. Before examining the assumptions and concepts on which I base this apparently outrageous claim, I give some examples of elementary teachers deciding to try it with children, and then I expand on this proposal. I try to convince the reader, with actual examples of what I consider to be impressive physics lessons, given the age of the students, that such a thing can really happen before I take up some of the deeper issues that such happenings raise.

CHILDREN EXPANDING ON WHAT TEACHERS READILY INITIATE THEMSELVES

I have been impressed with how much valuable activity happens spontaneously once a teacher starts encouraging pupils' thinking. For example, a kindergarten teacher who had seen a videotape of a third- and fourth-grade lesson in which children made predictions, observations, and then explanations, designed the following lesson for her class to follow the same structure.

She found five plastic margarine tubs and, with the point of a compass, punched one to five holes in the bottom of each. Both she and the children were surprised at their observation (contrary to their prediction) that no water leaked in when the tubs were set in an aquarium. One child suggested pressure was needed, and so they put counters they had on hand in each tub as weights until water began to enter the holes. Tabulation of the number of counters required for each different number of holes left them some doubt about their main hypothesis that the water would enter easier where there were more holes. Although the number of holes continued to hold their attention, they eventually discovered, to their surprise, that it took a certain depth of submersion to get the water to come through any of the holes. By directing the class to predict, observe, and explain, the teacher discovered that physics with children could be exciting, rewarding, and not as risky as she had feared.

At my suggestion, her fellow teachers, on learning about this experiment, tried filling the same tubs to various depths to see when the water first started coming out through the holes. It went on— another teacher tried using tubs with different sized holes in her class. As long as people are surprised and try to find out why, I suspect that conceptual progress is being made. But this is a case where children have a good deal of relevant experience to draw on; bathtub toys being one source. The child who said that pressure was probably needed was not just making a lucky guess. She must have had some experience in pressing something down to get water to enter it. There is a lot of follow through that can be done, tying into bouyancy and meterology. But I am content when teachers and children are engaged in processes of science like this without fears or tears. Frustration arises from trying to have all children reach the same concepts.

When teachers ask their pupils to try some of the popular elementary school science experiments (batteries and bulbs; candle in a jar; making a peeled, hardboiled egg go into a 1.5-inch neck bottle, etc.), there is plenty of excitement, but useful conceptual development by the children may be lacking when there is no discussion. I would like to encourage those experiments most and earliest where children make the best progress in conceptualization. Because that is difficult to judge in advance, I do not want to complain about pure fun. By progress, I do not mean, of course, that they rid themselves of all ideas that could conflict with later science lessons. What is important to conceptual progress is increasing openness to alternative conceptions and sharing ideas.

What if a teacher introduces students to a science activity that interests them but that does not stress concept development? For example, a first-grade teacher turned her class into a prediction and explanation lesson with students blowing through straws into a soap solution to make bubbles on their desk tops. The children could see if their predictions were true about blowing one bubble inside another, about penetrating a bubble without breaking it, about blowing bubbles on top of bubbles, and so on. Here, not much is identifiable in the way of traditional science concepts. However, rehearsal of the first two steps of the *prediction, observation, explanation* routine, with reports from each group, and group leader responsibilities in the clean-up is useful. Having well-established groups and carefully chosen leaders makes teaching so much easier, but it may not be considered fair to children who did not get chosen or do not like their group.

We really do not know when the specific experience with soap bubbles, which first-grade children obviously enjoy, will help them, but the social organization of the activity was surely valuable in a later lesson, perhaps with margarine tubs with holes in the bottom. Some children noticed colors on the bubbles, but explaining them was clearly out of reach. Some were reminded of the appearance of oil on a wet road—some pattern sensitivity is developing.

There was quite a bit more math and fun in another teacher-invented lesson: an ice melting race. Each group of children had an ice cube to try to melt in any way they could. The teacher kept time on each group from the simultaneous start to when each yelled, "It's gone." She then asked what the difference was between the fastest and slowest times, and a big problem developed for the third graders about borrowing minutes when subtracting minutes and seconds. Perhaps the math story problem that emerged was not related to the ideas about heat and melting that excited the children, but they did go back to the math problem again. Watching themselves on videotape renewed their motivation to do more work on borrowing seconds from the minutes column.

A combination science-physical education lesson measuring pulse rates over a period of time before and after exercising did not initially appear so valuable to me, but it seems to have paid off well for the fifth graders who did it. The teacher prepared a chart for them to enter daily records of heart rate before and after exercising. They came to understand how to judge their fitness over the 3 months it lasted, and even noticed a slump over their 1-week spring break. Practice in multiplying pulse counts per 15 seconds by 4 in their heads did not hurt their math, and some averaging was done, too.

An impressive example of the prediction, observation, and explanation approach is known as "smart marbles." When marbles of uniform size roll down a track and collide with a stationary row of similar marbles, the same number roll off the far end of the row as came down the track and hit the near end. How do those at the far end know what happened at the near end? They must be "smart marbles." Children invent many variations.

With quotations from 28 children in "stage II," Piaget (1972), in collaboration with Alina Szeminska, showed how creatively children of elementary school age can think about the phenomenon. Piaget and Szeminska seemed to have been looking for the Newtonian action = reaction formulation—doubtless to prove to empiricists, who could not see how invisible causal agents could be known from observation of nature, that Kant was right: Mental schemes available to everyone (at least, nearly everyone above the age of 10) permit perception of the causality Newton saw. As an educator, I cannot help being impressed with alternative theories expressed in the dialogues between children talking about "smart marbles" in the classroom. The children's ideas covered the subject well, and their formulations of ideas improved greatly during the 45 minutes devoted to it.

Piaget (1972) gave many examples of the transmission of a chain of collisions theory including this one in which I have coded each utterance as participating in or evoking one of the prediction, observation, explanation processes (coded P, O, or E):

One active marble rolls down a slope and strikes the end of a row of marbles on a flat, felt mat (see Fig. 3.1).

O   ALV (9;2), six marbles in the row: There are all the others which go ahead.

E   INT: How?

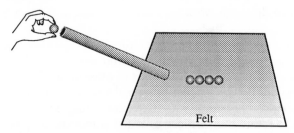

FIG. 3.1.   Apparatus used by Alina Szeminska for experiment (Piaget, 1972).

P   ALV: [Points to the last one and beyond the line and 45 degrees to the left or the right.]

P   INT: Are they going far?

E   ALV: If that hits harder it goes farther.

E   INT: What is going to make it hit?

E   ALV: It is the impulse of the marble. [One marble is released down the slope.]

O   ALV: The impulse gave a tap and the last one left.

O   INT: And the others?

O   ALV: They are staying.

O   INT: Did they move or not?

O   ALV: They moved a little.

O   INT: How much?

E   ALV: Each one hit after the other and after the last (next to the last), and the other (the last one) left . . . They have each moved one marble ahead: that one (next to the last) replaces that one (the last), since that one replaced that one (etc., moving one step for each one).

O   INT: Look!

O   ALV: No, that one hasn't moved.

E   INT: Then?

E   ALV: They tap it a little but don't move (it), they give it impulse.

P   INT: And with nine?

P   ALV: One is going to leave like before.

P   INT: And with four?

PE   ALV: The fewer marbles there are, the more impulse they have for leaving. (pp. 78–79, my translation)

There are two clearly distinct and apparently conflicting explanations that emerge from this interview and also in the several classes of children (Grades 3 to 7) who have studied the "smart marbles." The first that ALV mentions is the chain of speed-exchange collisions leading the last marble to leave alone. Many children see that this chain action is repeated for each active marble. The other is a conservation law: The marbles moving down the track have just enough of a quantity of motion (variously called *force, energy, power, strength*) to knock off the same number of marbles from the end of the stationary row. (A dictionary could help children say which definitions of these words they like best.) In ALV, at the end, something like the momentum of the initially active marble(s) sets a limit, within which "number" (mass?) and "impulse" are inversely related.

In high school and college textbooks, on the other hand, the simpler phenomenon with a row of swinging balls is sometimes explained as

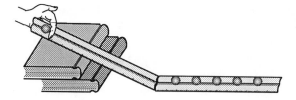

FIG. 3.2.   Separating the stationary marbles to watch chain of collision.

conservation of momentum (mv) and/or conservation of energy (1/2 mv²). Although the "smart marbles" fit a conservation law, such a law is neither necessary nor sufficient to explain their behavior. Few children speak of the conservation of number of balls that are moving before and after the collision. Even those who do not know the formula for momentum, with its mass-velocity trade off, often know that they should test a more massive marble, to see if it generates enough of some quantity of motion to knock off several little ones at the other end. Some discover other interesting places to place a more massive marble in the apparatus, and some experiment with separating the stationary marbles, so they "can see what is really happening" (see Fig. 3.2).

A debate among third and fourth graders, after 45 minutes of studying "smart marbles," reached this point:

Brad: When she (Erin) said that one marble only had enough power to just move one marble. . . . How could that one marble make all them other marbles to make the last marble move? (See Fig. 3.3.)

Teacher: Ok, how does that one marble have enough power to move all the other marbles?

Samantha: It goes fast.

Teacher: It moves fast when you let go.

Brad: Do you agree with Erin . . . that . . . ?

Ronald: Even if it could go, it doesn't go fast.

Brad: Put it at the top.

Teacher: Ok, put it at the top of the ruler.

Brad: How did that one marble make all those other marbles move, to make just that last marble move? [Conservation,

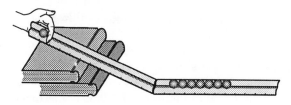

FIG. 3.3.   Releasing one marble against a compact row of marbles.

interpreted just as equality of input and output, still seems unbelievable to Brad, who earlier had advanced a blow-by-blow transmission account of the chain of collisions started by each approaching marble.]

Ronald: This one marble has the strength to move this one marble, and this one marble has the strength, and it goes on and on. [So conservation is assumed to work at the level of the invisible interactions between single marbles.]

Brad: I agree with Ronald.

Teacher: Ok! Group Number Three.

Travis: If you put a space between each marble . . . like the amount you have at the top [pause]. . . . then one less marble comes off at the end. [This opens up the debate all over again.]

It strikes me as interesting that, although individuals are working out their own ideas and how to say them, no general consensus is emerging yet, although Brad has conceded to Ronald that conservation of "strength" from one-marble-to-the-next makes sense. The teacher, in concentrating as she did throughout on getting everyone to express their ideas, has no doubt greatly facilitated this scientific debate. She plays the role of a master of ceremonies, not a scientific participant, for which she lacks the confidence of her beliefs (compared, e.g., with Brad, Erin, and Ronald). To expect everyone in a scientific society meeting to agree on one general conclusion would be premature and it is clearly premature here—nor did an agreement emerge during the reports of Groups 4 and 5 before the class period ended. However, some pupils did refer back to "smart marbles" a week or two later, suggesting that they shared a common understanding about them.

I usually like to listen to dialogues between several children better than listening to interview dialogues. Children engaged in a peer-group dialogue often work harder on the meanings of words and experimental issues than they do when talking with an adult.

A PROBLEM ABOUT CHILDREN'S IDEAS
THAT THIS PROPOSAL RAISES

We have seen some science tasks for which the intellectual resources of the children themselves appear to be sufficient for them to make sound educational progress. But the question still remains: Should children be expected to draw enough useful science concepts from their own resources so that teachers could set aside altogether instructing them in the accepted concepts? It required centuries of intellectual struggle for most current scientific concepts to emerge in the community of scientists (or mathematicians). To many people, asking children to reinvent all the ideas they need to learn about science seems ridiculous. When children enter school they have already learned a great deal of their native language, reinventing meanings for the words they have heard around them, with better results I suppose than if someone had tried to teach those meanings to them, but that accomplishment is easy to overlook.

I first saw the possibility that children could reinvent a lot of elementary physics concepts in 1968. Piaget was engaged in studies of 5- to 14-year-old children's causal reasoning for 100 different mechanics and heat experiments. I heard about half of the research reports in weekly seminars of Le Centre Internationale d'Epistémologie Génétique and read them over and over, and observed a dozen or more interviews conducted at school and discussed the results afterwards with the interviewers. Thirty-five studies were published in French and a brief synopsis of each of the 100 was included in a book by Piaget and Garcia (1974). In all, except one on magnets that was included to prove the point that children lacked the experiential basis for magnetic concepts, the progress from 5 to 14 was remarkable among these children from the working class, who were noticeably ahead of any schooling they had in physics. These studies, so much more optimistic than Piaget's studies with Inhelder, for which Piaget is best known, influenced his subsequent research in the last decade of his life. One, published the year he died (1980) reports children's explanations of the mysterious "drinking bird" sometimes seen in notions stores.

Other researchers have shown conflicts between children's preconceptions and the intended instruction (Driver et al., 1985), which require explanation. The concepts children express in thinking about physical phenomena are, as I suggested earlier, very sensitive to the context in which they are used, including the prior uses they themselves have been making. When interviewers from Piaget's team asked them to predict, observe, and explain the tasks Piaget chose, children appeared to think more like physicists than when many of these other researchers asked them to express their ideas about forces and motion. Electrical circuits do not seem to be their cup of tea, but electrical transmission systems are (Driver et al., 1985, chapter 3). $f = ma$ is not children's universal law of motion, but motion transmission is (see p. 69). At times, even Piaget had difficulty accepting the validity of the children's ideas, as he admits in *Understanding Causality*. For example, he reluctantly accepted the validity of a child's explanation of the motion of a released balloon, that the air inside was in two parts: one part pushing the balloon ahead and the other part pushing itself out of the neck of the balloon. So, when the neck is released the balloon is moved (Piaget & Garcia, 1974, p. 74). Perhaps most science educators who study such conflicts between alternative and standard explanatory principles have not listened enough to children's explanations to appreciate them and the links they make with breakthroughs in the history of science (Driver et al., 1985, pp. 197ff).

In order for children's untutored conceptualizations to surface, a flexibility and openness of mind that our educational system does not generally encourage may be required. I can only infer that, although some children were trying to absorb passively what they were being taught, and still others were abandoning science forever, the critical and creative thinkers, even as small children, practiced a skeptical attitude. At least privately, they were challenging everything that teachers and textbooks had to say.

Their creative abilities are even more impressive to me than their critical ones. Consider the following example:

Two fifth-grade girls working on the "smart marbles" phenomena, said they had "weighed" marbles by making one collide with an other of a different size.

Teacher: Explain that a little bit more, when you were talking about the power.

Robin: The power . . .

Maura: When it rolls down it gets faster, so it has more force. When it rolls down, the gravity pulls it, so it goes faster and faster. If you watch a marble go down . . . If you watch it, it goes real fast. And how fast it goes, it gets more power as it rolls down. If you're running . . . If you run and push somebody, you get more power then, 'cause you're gaining, than if you're standing behind someone and just push someone. You get more. You're getting ready for it, you know (gestures pushing].

*Teacher: Momentum?

Maura: and so . . .

Teacher: Now, how did you compare that with the big one?

Maura: What do you mean?

Teacher: Well, you were comparing the small size with the bigger marble.

Maura: this . . .

Teacher: I thought you tried with the small marble and then with the bigger marble.

Maura: Like this?

Teacher: Uh huh.

Maura: Well . . .

Teacher: And you said something about the weight of the larger marble.

Maura: Well, here . . . [She experiments, rolling a large marble down to hit a row of four small marbles.] It pushes so many down with its force. When this [small one] gains [by rolling down the slope], it gets about double its power, which is about this size [big one]. But when this [big one] rolls, it gets double its power, which is about this big [gesture showing sphere about 4 inches across], so it has so much power it can push. How many pushes that would probably mean, how much power it has, how much weight it has, so . . .

Teacher: Robin, what do you think?

Robin: Well, we . . . I think the same

Maura: It pushed four.

Robin: Yeah, because four began to come off, but then . . .

You see at the asterisk that the teacher's guidance is ignored. Maura is struggling to find suitable words. But her idea comes through nevertheless: Mass and speed almost trade off as in momentum.

Here, again, I see a child producing better explanations than those usually found in physics textbooks. To many science educators, this could be a doubly shocking charge. First, it elevates a crude piece of childish intuition, and second, it degrades principles derived from Newton's laws. It deserves some documentation.

This child had earlier described a dominoe-like chain of collisions, started by the active marble, as a detailed transmission mechanism. It often develops that such a mechanism is considered sufficient to explain the rule that the same number comes off one end as hits the other (one comes off for each chain), but many children appeal to a conservation law. Not Maura! She saw no need for it. She was, however, intrigued by the larger marble and worked on the relationship between size and speed, recognizing a trade off, as ALV had done in the previous example.

In Newtonian mechanics, several laws could be applied. For example, conservation of momentum (mass × velocity) and conservation of energy (half the mass × its velocity^2). Each such law reports that a given function of mass and velocities in some frame of reference is unchanged by elastic collisions, so no one of them alone can explain the fact that the impact of a gently rolling, larger marble will just knock one marble off the end of a stationary row. Two or more such laws must be combined algebraically to calculate the resulting velocity. However, understanding such collisions geometrically and mechanically requires more than algebra. Understanding of the results of such calculations usually requires dozens of applications of these laws to various systems in the laboratory and many more problems approached theoretically. Marbles are more complex than the swinging steel balls because rotational inertia is generated and, most of the time, all the marbles move a little. That point, however, is apparently not picked up by most of the students in my observations in classrooms. Few students in introductory physics courses understand these laws well enough to grasp why one moving marble (of different mass) hitting a row of equal masses gently, makes just one go off. However, children's chain of collision mechanism, ignoring mass and velocity, always requires the last marble in a chain of collisions to leave reference (Piaget & Garcia, 1974, pp. 12ff).

Even the law of velocity symmetry in the center of mass frame of reference, does not account for the fact that two marbles hitting a third one make two separate collisions (and make two marbles move away), whereas a single marble twice the other's mass can produce only one collision (and only one marble flies off).

Most textbooks require too much sophistication to be helpful here. For example, Ganot (1873, pp. 33–34) presented one of Newton's experiments with two suspended colliding balls and explained it by conservation of momentum and a geometrical derivation based on conservation of kinetic and potential energy in a pendulum. Tipler (1976) used classical relativity to change frames of reference and derive the relation between velocities in an elastic collision of unequal masses. Neither raise the question of multiple, linear collisions at all. However, Lemon and Ference's monumental text (1946, pp. 53–55) comes closest, presenting a full, illustrated discussion of the phenomenon. It then, includes the following problem about a collider with larger mass: "what would you think would happen if (1) a single ball of twice the mass of the others strikes the row?" Clearly, $mv = constant$ is consistent with either one ball leaving with twice the velocity or two balls leaving with the same velocity, so some other information is needed. It becomes clear that conservation must be computed separately on each collision, too difficult a task for physics textbooks to treat.

In the philosophers' and scientists' emphasis on formal laws and their application, the role of underlying mechanisms is often neglected. Harré (1972) is one of just a handful of philosophers and historians who emphasize the importance of underlying mechanisms in scientific explanations instead of pretending that the formal laws themselves are sufficient. Textbook authors are usually not trying to give the best explanation of each phenomenon, but choose phenomena that are the best examples of the explanatory principles they want to illustrate. When the pupil explains the phenomenon differently from the text, it does not at all mean it is wrong. It may even be better than what the text gave. Teachers who insist on judging each explanation right or wrong often have an unreasonable task on their hands. But a skeptic insists some scientist invented and tried out each valid idea a pupil can offer and, textbook or no, there must be a way to evaluate them by current theory.

Conceptualization is not the exclusive business of scholarship. Piaget and Garcia (1983) argued that children face the same crises of ideology (e.g., whether the world is basically static or dynamic) that the intellectual communities responsible for Western science faced, and that children deal with them in much the same way. That, they conclude, is why they sometimes seem to recapitulate a scientific discovery of an earlier age in their own thinking. (Apelman, Flexer, Carlson, & Hawkins, 1983; Hanson, 1984, provide interesting views on this question.)

Perhaps because children have so often been observed conceptualizing phenomena in domains where their experience provides them with useful metaphors, the contribution of the creative scientist needs to be seen in a different role. Instead of thinking of creative scientists primarily as inventors of new concepts that no one ever had before, they should be thought of as selecting the most promising concept for a given purpose from wherever they can find it, even, according to my conjecture, from their own childhood repertory of concepts. Once a concept is selected, the creative scientist then faces the most demanding task of all, for which a sophisticated acquaintance with science is essential: Expressing it in terms that other scientists can understand, appreciate, and use. For example, we thank Feynmann for Feynmann Diagrams, not for the idea of causal trains they represent, and we thank Newton for his law of gravity, not for the idea of action at a distance.

Some philosophers and historians of science have come close to recognizing this selective role of the scientist. Thus, Holton and Roller (1958) said, "The lesson to be derived from history is that *science as a structure grows by a struggle for survival among ideas*—that there are marvelous processes at work which in time purify the meanings even of initially confused concepts" (p. 232). Jammer (1957) described Galileo as "grappling with an intuitive notion of force and searching for an exact formulation" (p. 95). He then listed Italian expressions Galileo used (*forza, potenze, virtu, possanza, momento della potenza*) but said Galileo preferred *impeto*, and illustrated how he used terms such as these in the following quotation:

When one holds a stone in his hand does he do anything but give it a force impelling (*virtu impellente*) it upwards equal to the power (*facolta*) of gravity drawing it downwards? And do you not continuously impress this force (*virtu*) upon the stone as long as you hold it in the hand? . . . . From these considerations it appears to me that we may obtain a proper solution of the problem discussed by philosophers, namely, what causes the acceleration in the natural motion of heavy bodies. (Galileo, quoted in Jammer, 1957, p. 100)

Ziman (1968) wrote:

Some men are very learned, able to bring to mind a relevant fact or notion on any subject, repositories of wisdom for their students and contemporaries. Although inhibited from imaginative steps by their attachment to existing knowledge, they are the safe moorings from which more lively craft venture forth. Some are very imaginative, having a hundred new ideas a day, of which ninety are patent nonsense, another nine are eventually found wrong and the remaining one is a winner. (p. 80)

These quotations and perhaps Piaget and Garcia too suggest that the scholars who made the initial breakthroughs in mechanics were able to try out many ideas including those common to the children of any era, who at age 9 or 10 are often making preliminary formulations of mechanical concepts. Once the ideological and other constraints have been released, the source of the new ideas is immaterial.

Jammer (1961) said:

The quantity of matter present in a body determines, according to Buridan and his school, quite generally the resistance that a physical object exerts against the moving force. Although resistance here, as in Aristotle, is still considered a real force, it is surprising to see how closely the impetus theory approached the concept of inertial mass. But impetus was not momentum and resistance not inertia. (p. 50)

When a kindergarten child, seeing the perforated plastic tub floating on the water with no leakage, cried out, "It needs pressure," and that word was interpreted in terms of putting objects in the tub, we see clearly that this use of "pressure" was plausible. Knowing something about mechanics, we can see that the objects' action on the water is distributed over the area of the bottom of the tub (which is almost one of the definitions of pressure), and we can see the resistance the holes offer to the passage of the water as the interesting part of the counter pressure to be overcome (which differs little from surface tension)

Pressures in opposition, equilibrium, and disequilibrium, are also in evidence. (A big dictionary can be helpful again, because in fluid mechanics, "pressure" is omnidirectional, but not in all English language usage.) But, naturalistically speaking, liquids are not completely compliant to every little action on them. We must sometimes press them, or suck on them, to get them to go where we want, so the word "pressure" comes to mind. Words heard in the speech environment must be tried out.

The teacher, no physicist, who was surprised herself that even the tub with five holes was not leaking, was impressed both by the word "pressure" and the request for weights from her 5-year-old students. Clearly, the children succeeded with these initiatives addressed to their teacher who was doing the experiment for them while they watched. But isn't this science, and successful science, on the part of the teacher and the children? Does this not mean that when the conditions are right, people (from 5 to 105) will do "good" science? Perhaps especially if they help each other in small groups! Secondary school science teachers will recognize that Pascal's Law that fluid pressure acts equally in all directions, is still not appreciated. There is much to learn about pressure, but with this teacher, there may be many more opportunities.

SOME ELEMENTARY TEACHERS' PERSPECTIVES ON SCIENCE TEACHING

Many of the teachers' concerns were not so evident as the fundamental issue discussed in the last section. It took me several years to begin to understand the issue of teacher authority in their terms. My first idea, that teachers felt nervous not controlling their pupils' thoughts and guiding them toward the official right responses, has not survived intact during the 7 or 8 years I have spent working with teachers and future teachers. To be sure, there was evidence of that, but there was also evidence of nervousness about not understanding the official textbook explanations of scientific phenomena.

My puzzlement as to why teachers resist and struggle with the desired epistemological conversion received some new light recently in an elementary science methods course I was teaching with Bernadine Evans Stake, using as a textbook, Driver et al. (1985).

The students in the course worked 9 weeks in an elementary classroom during the mid-part of the course, and as usual in my class, they were asked to try peer-group dialogues. Most of them reported the children were much more interested and involved in the peer-group dialogues than in presentations or discussions guided toward a standard answer. They could also see from the text that their own ideas about physical phenomena were close to some of those identified as common preconceptions. They were amazed at the variety of different ideas reported in their text on each phenomenon, and they could see that children in their classes had even more ideas than the text reported.

Soon we began to hear them say to each other and report to us that they had said to their pupils, "In science, there are no right and wrong answers." Bernadine and I queried them about what they meant, disavowing any claims that we had said anything so sweeping. Written, ungraded quizzes called for their explanation of the statement, and the final exam asked for an explanation of a scenario involving two apparent contradictions of that statement.

At this writing, I am not at all sure I understand this phenomenon, but I offer the following interpretation as something better than anything I have understood before on the general question of teacher authority.

William Perry (1970) made the case that many students come to undergraduate university study with a firm attachment to "dualism," and that, only with great reluctance, will they abandon their belief that there are right answers for every question, that other answers are wrong, and that the teacher's job is to teach the right ones and correct students when they give the wrong ones. As conscientious students, of course, they are trying to find out what the right answers are and avoid giving wrong ones. Perry and Whitlock (1954) have reported that undergraduates who learned critical reading skills from clinical tutoring remember their assignments better if they are critical than if they read passively. But the students were often so shocked at this insight they became depressed over the way they had "wasted their whole lives" by only studying passively. To prevent such depression, Perry and Whitlock provided subsequent tutees with a reading pacer, as a placebo, so it would receive the credit for the students' improved performance instead of their perception of a "simple" switch in reading style. Perry (1970) gave nine stages in the development of relativism.

Giving up dualism is obviously painful, and our students may have discovered another way out. Studying and hearing children's alternative ideas about scientific phenomena, and hearing criticisms from Bernadine Stake and me of the glib overgeneralizations often found in science textbooks may have induced an instant relativism painlessly. That is, they saw that children's ideas change as do scientists', and they can only change theirs with hard thinking that is not guaranteed to lead them to the official answer, so they as teachers are relieved of the awful responsibility of having to say which answers are right and which are wrong. The children can decide for themselves, as research suggests they are doing anyway, and they love it. In responding to another question on the final examination, in which they had to recommend how to finish a lesson (whose beginning they were given in 3 minutes of video and 6 minutes of transcript) they often admired, without solicitation, the artful way the teacher asked questions that gave none of the clues teachers are wont to give about what the right answers might be. They said, "In science there are no right or wrong answers."

Further insight into the awesome responsibility teachers and future teachers may feel to say what is right and wrong comes from the responses our students made to our efforts to confront the undergraduates with counter examples to this sweeping overgeneralization, far removed from anything the authors of their text intended.

In the scenario on the methods course exam, a child taunted by a peer because his prediction had been wrong by observation, quoted the teacher that there are no right or wrong answers. Although most of the 60 students recognized that predictions could turn out to be right or wrong, some did not, developing two main defenses. First, some argued that one observation could not disprove anything; many observations were needed. The second was to argue, in a fashion reminiscent of the concept of theory-laden data advanced by N. R. Hanson (1958), that predictions that seemed to be disproved by evidence interpreted today might turn out to be acceptable tomorrow, presumably when people's ideas have changed. Neither they nor we have seen such a case with children's predictions and observations. Although pupils may sometimes challenge the evidence, not recognizing that they collect evidence in theory-laden ways, the child of the scenario, who used the teacher's statement to defend his disproved prediction, was recognized by some of our students as either a fiction or as having a very extreme case of teacher dependency.

We are left with the task of helping teachers face the reality of conceptual change through finding out what is right and wrong through investigation.

CRITICAL THINKING IN ELEMENTARY
SCHOOL SCIENCE

Science in the elementary school curriculum has had a varied tradition, ranging from nature study to the introduction of sophisticated conceptual "inventions" like *relative motion* and *system interaction*

(Robert Karplus' Science Curriculum Improvement Study). And there is no doubt that many children, teachers, and parents may take pride when their children learn the names of organs of the human body; the names of dinosaurs, snakes, insects; and recognize trees by the shapes of their leaves. I do not want to put down nominalistic science entirely, because there is always the possibility for pupil's critical thought and creativity even there (e.g., noticing variation in leaf shape with the age of the leaf, etc.). On the other hand, I have seen boxes of inquiry science kits permanently stored in many elementary school closets, presumably because of lack of teacher confidence in using them.

There are increasing numbers of jobs that require critical thinking and fewer and fewer jobs on which following directions blindly is expected. However, I have yet to see a page in an elementary school science textbook that could not benefit from children's common sense criticism. There are usually oversimplifications and errors of oversight, to be found in both the illustrations and the text, which some children in any class will be able to find, and apparent conflicts arising because of the naturally ambiguous language we speak, as well as mistaken portrayals of the scientific enterprise itself. (See, "The Exception Improves the Rule" section later.) Furthermore, the more authoritative the text in elementary school the greater the probability that children will become over anxious about conflicts between their own ideas of the world and the school subjects associated with science.

I do not expect nonspecialized elementary school teachers to judge the scientific merits of elementary textbooks or the ideas that the children themselves express in the same way as would those professional science educators and others who have been studying children's own ideas (Driver, 1983; Driver et al., 1985; West & Pines, 1985). They have documented dozens of standard science concepts that are in conflict with students' ideas, even after years of specific instruction in high school or college. Most elementary school teachers have had few opportunities to master standard science concepts. Furthermore, science methods texts provide no opportunity to understand the literature on children's ideas in science.

Until a few years ago, my own expectations were similar to those of most science educators, but they resulted in my general discouragement as a teacher educator. What I now believe teachers should do about the conflicts between texts and children's ideas in the classroom is to engage the students in making comparisons between their own views and what they interpret the text to be saying. That is, teachers should promote *critical reading*, as described on p. 79 of this chapter. (For examples of elementary science text criticism, see folk science formulas 2, 3, 8, 10, 11, 13, 15, 17, 20, and 21, on pp. 89-91 of this chapter.)

Many educators also expect teachers to provide so-called "hands-on" or "discovery" experiences in science. These, unfortunately, are usually interpreted as ways of arriving at correct conclusions. Elementary teachers can easily become discouraged in teaching science—they have difficulty finding equipment, the experiments do not work reliably, planning takes an unreasonable amount of time, the school day is crowded, classroom management seems more difficult when children become excited, and children's ideas turn out, on examination, to be either wrong but resistant to change, or nearly right but disguised by language.

In view of teachers' salaries and the working conditions in the schools, I do not expect to find amateur scientists there. Science enthusiasts can find much better pay and working conditions elsewhere. Teachers who work with 30 children all day, if they had professional-level mastery of science and all the subjects of the elementary school, would competitively have to be paid $60,000 and be provided with a staff of assistants. Now I usually recommend the second alternative mentioned earlier—the promotion of children's science, which I often enjoy much more than when I was taking the first approach as a science enthusiast teacher, promoting the science that I had learned or that I was learning. I am pleased to find teachers who share this interest in children's science who do not share my enthusiasm for adult science learning. However, I find teachers who develop superior teaching abilities in elementary and middle schools wondering seriously if they can put up indefinitely with the lack of appreciation for pupil thinking by their fellow teachers and their administrators. They need to be part of a more concerted movement to tolerate the stress.

After 12 years of working closely with a few dozen elementary school teachers, the careful study of videotapes of children working productively on conceptually difficult science problems seems the best way to generate enthusiasm for children's science—for giving them the possibilities of thinking. By analyzing the shifting meanings of words in the language of individual pupils and groups in a videotaped lesson, teachers and future teachers can develop sensitivity to children's science dialogues and realization of the difficulty most adults face in guiding them. A number of such teachers have become promoters of using dictionaries' alternative meanings to overcome their anxieties about "unscientific" uses of words.

If I try, as I often have, to engage teachers or future teachers in a simulation of children's science enquiries, they complain because I will not give them the answers they seek, and I complain because they are so much more inhibited than children. However, if no recording is being made, they often create just as good explanations and produce almost as good criticisms as children do, showing that the authoritarian science teaching they have experienced has not completely debilitated their creative and critical abilities.

If most teachers have other much higher priorities than personally becoming involved in science, their pupils need not be poorly educated in science. The theoretical and analytical resources children have themselves are adequate for a very strong elementary school science study, although perhaps some curriculum adjustment will be needed. There are lots of good materials, and when teachers begin to look for them, I hope someone will help them to find them. The Elementary Science Study is still one of the best.

Children's ideas about collisions and some other aspects of mechanics seem more advanced (in spite of their belief, notorious among researchers, that motion always requires a force) than they are in the more traditional subjects of elementary school science like plant and animal physiology and meterology. This is completely plausible in light of children's daily encounters involving motion. Work in this natural area could perhaps compensate for the lesser interest most elementary teachers show in mechanics than they show in aspects of biology, chemistry, and electricity, where children's experiences are usually more limited.

Teachers usually know how to manage social arrangements that ensure that all children have opportunities to think. But they wouldn't think of using them when trying to get everyone to "the right answer." However, the results in pupils' knowledge attained and in their aroused interest can be impressive, and elementary school teachers would be the first to notice and appreciate them. As examples given earlier in this chapter illustrate, the levels of competency that fourth- or fifth-grade children are likely to attain in some areas of mechanics, for example, can be far higher than most junior high programs now expect, because they now presume little or no background for such topics. On the other hand, junior high school programs expect more students to like science than actually do, by the time they reach seventh grade.

American educators interested in school reform are often complacent about the elementary science curriculum, as well as about mathematical problem solving, because in the United States we produce outstanding scientists and engineers, and a substantial group of science fans, who, although not practicing scientists, manage to keep up with some of the more exciting developments in science. Although students from Asia and Europe attending U.S. graduate schools make very impressive marks in science and mathematics tests, American scientists may still hold the creative edge. But strong forces in Japan are seeking to enhance the creativity in Japanese schools (Marshall, 1986).

I wonder if the creative edge of American science is not partly due to the subtle resistance of the 5%–10% of independent thinkers among our school population against the general pressure to conformity (Grieb & Easley, 1984). In my visits to schools, I regularly find one or two children in nearly every elementary school classroom who are educating themselves well in science, who take their own initiatives to think over the explanations given, to look for contrary evidence, and even to criticize their own explanations for inconsistencies. Whatever the internal or external sources of their creative and critical abilities may be, they seem to take the usual authoritarian positions of teachers and texts as personally challenging.

Many of the top graduates of universities and colleges, who specialized in a science, report having had such an independent attitude during their elementary school years. This raises the possibility that authoritarian presentation of science that has, with every good intention, been simplified too much for today's children, may be a major factor contributing to this country's production of leading scientists. Pressure for conformity, however, does not seem helpful in generating the numbers of creative and critical thinkers our "high tech" society needs. Because universal school reform is not possible, one could ask whether there is a minimum schedule of classes or tutoring that encourages critical thinking in science for all pupils, with most of the work done in authoritarian classes that cannot tolerate it openly. Clearly, there is too little control for anyone to effect such a design if they knew what it was and wanted to do it. Following 7 children who had a lot of critical experience in the third and fourth grade found no spontaneous uses in 3 more years of conventional schooling (Easley & Sekita, 1989). Could young children benefit from a brief encouragement in creative and critical reactions to authoritarian science lessons? Would it enhance the appreciation and use of science in ordinary business and industrial jobs (where the overall quality of work in the United States is too often low by European and Japanese standards)? One or two changed teachers may be all we could reasonably hope for in most schools until we can develop a critical mass of teachers who support thinking. Can children encountering only an occasional, enriched science class benefit when they return to the more conventional mix? It seems plausible, on the evidence of mathematics tests, that even 1 or 2 years of challenging experience as young children can boost computation, problem solving, and concept scores for 3 successive years, even if no other changes occur in their schooling (Easley & Sekita, 1989).

Specific, and very practical, advice over several years is needed for those teachers who would like to help their pupils benefit from what they may have lacked themselves in the way of an elementary scientific education.

I estimate roughly that more than 50% of U.S. elementary school teachers, mainly by their own choice, teach little or no science in their classrooms. Of those, perhaps less than half would take the initiative to do so, if given a program they considered practical. The priorities of the others are different. Many of those who are already trying would probably be open to something that works even better, for the future well-being of their students in an age of science must be one of their greatest concerns. The rest would be inclined, I suspect, to wait and see what happens with those who try.

A PRACTICAL SOLUTION FOR TEACHERS INTERESTED IN MINDS-ON SCIENCE

Pupil's motivation for critical investigation of challenging problems at times seems automatic, but it may be quite uneven in some classes. A little dramatization, playing the devil's advocate, or other theatrics may be called for by the teacher at the beginning or when one group lags. They should be allowed to "go at it" independently, to develop their confidence and courage (which may have been lost in previous schooling or at home), and to learn to enjoy surprises and consider different ideas instead of depending on the teacher for closure.

Some formal social structure of the class is needed to provide ample thinking opportunity for all pupils in large classes (15 +), and to help teachers who lack confidence in this approach. To organize classes into semipermanent heterogeneous groups for sharing ideas seems to be a very effective way. This is different from lab groups where all work as a team and reports tend to be identical. From time to time during a class, the individual work of the pupils can be shared with members of their group. Group leaders may be trained to give every pupil in the group support for expressing their ideas and receiving criticism from their peers. An oral report on the new ideas each group discussion produces should be given to the class with opportunity for questions from the class.

It is also very practical to have groups perform experiments, make observations, and even to devise their own experiments. The teacher's role here becomes one of first presenting a challenging problem and then moderating the discussion, asking for minority reports from a group that had a division of opinion and modeling the role of "chair" for the group leaders. Clearly, many teachers will want a collection of sufficiently challenging problems, although some teachers have found that pupils can produce enough on their own.

An opinion poll on a scientific debate is very useful to ensure total class participation and keep track of shifting trends of thought. Since Thomas Kuhn's (1961) *Structure of Scientific Revolutions*, it has been clear that the evolution of scientific knowledge involves social decisions about which available conceptual systems are most profitable. Lakatos (1977, 1979) described debates over which research program is most progressive. Only within a paradigm or research program can a particular piece of evidence settle any issues. Between paradigms a social decision is in order but rational arguments, such as where the preponderance of evidence lies, are still relevant matters. Children are going through debates between paradigms in all the problems investigated and they deserve to know the drift of opinion as well as the evidence.

Questions teachers ask me when introduced to the aforementioned steps are as follows:

- How do you organize effective discussion groups?
- What if the children don't reach a general explanation that all agree on by the end of the period?
- What do we do next?
- How do we know when we have finished with a topic?
- What will the parents say if they hear that the teacher is not giving out any answers?

In discussions with U.S. teachers about these topics, I sometimes drew heavily on practices some Japanese teachers had developed, and sometimes they were based entirely on the U.S. teachers' own experiences. Videotapes of Japanese and U.S. classes were often useful in suggesting some detailed way in which depending on peer-group dialogue can be found to work.

What about social and communication conventions?

From videotapes, other teachers pick up many solutions to technical problems about different arrangements of furniture, managing a discussion, and so forth.

THE EXCEPTION (IM)PROVES THE RULE

The proposal I have just made entails that teachers who accept it actually reclaim their traditional authority role regarding science by promoting science reasoning processes (prediction, observation, explanation, evaluating evidence, making analogies, and devising other experiments) and fostering communication skills (speaking clearly and with confidence, listening, taking turns, etc.). These processes and skills are necessary in order to facilitate pupils' study of science through peer-group dialogues. This proposal raises serious conceptual difficulties for traditional views of science and education.

I am persuaded by Lakatos (1977) that looking for exceptions is a major way scientists and mathematicians, as well as pupils, improve their theories. As a social scientist, I think that is also a good way to improve my theory of teaching and learning. Frankly, I keep finding exceptions to other peoples' rules. Other educators, in authoritative tones, affirm their fears about peer-group dialogue. For example, one educator responded, "We are told that teachers need only communication skills when in fact they need conceptual knowledge for analyzing teaching and learning." Another said, "In my view any such attempt to improve the training of elementary teachers must also be buttressed by formal attention to the transmission of mathematical and science content." I am trying to find ways to do this without promoting authoritarianism. I face a dilemma: Do I argue for my own beliefs on the basis of my beliefs or build on teachers' beliefs to try to persuade them of my own? I think the answer is that I must try to do both, but separately.

I want teachers to explore what children are capable of accomplishing and to reconsider their typical authoritarian patterns and what their students are actually accomplishing. How much teachers change their practices is their responsibility. I am trying to examine what changes they do make and what the effects are with or without conceptual changes in science on their part. Doing so generates numerous counter examples to almost anyone's list of what teachers need themselves, or what they need to do in order to succeed in improving the problem-solving and conceptual development of their pupils.

I think that our schools will recognize a more professionally responsible stance by teachers, when teachers turn away from conceptual goals to thinking processes. First, I propose to consider one of the prevailing conceptions of science among teachers of elementary grades and how it could be criticized to improve children's creative and critical thinking. Paradoxically, this conception can best be criticized by inviting children to criticize science authorities to see if they do not learn more of what the authorities say than if they try to accept them uncritically.

Science for elementary school children is traditionally focused on learning expressions that have the form of generalizations such as, "hot air rises," "like poles of magnets repel and unlike poles attract," or "plants need water, sunshine, soil and air." Of course, there is usually a particular context in which these generalizations are taught— a demonstration, an experiment, or observations that are supposed to suggest the generalization. Children may have other generalizations they apply in those contexts, and most children will also have some experience, in or out of school, that conflicts with one of these generalizations or with an understandable interpretation of it. Furthermore, the interpretations will differ from child to child. If the children's experiences were pooled, nearly all the generalizations would be subject to serious questioning by someone in the room.

When children learn that "we breathe in oxygen and breathe out carbon dioxide," they often need to have these words interpreted for them so they do not think it means that what enters our trachaeas from the outside is pure oxygen and that what comes out of our trachaeas through our nostrils or mouth is pure carbon dioxide. Misinterpretations of such formulas by children are common, and most university science students, researchers have found, hold some such misinterpretations. Inevitably, elementary school teachers, themselves, do also, because they usually studied science without taking a very critical stance. Furthermore, most achievement tests are not designed with any reference to the literature on children's preconceptions, so they cannot discriminate between the different meanings words can have, as though each word had only one.

In elementary science texts, as in the culture, there are simpler versions of many science formulas for young children and more complex versions for students in higher grades. In so far as these formulas constitute a traditional curriculum which many parents and others expect to appear in certain versions for certain grades, they deserve to be called "folk science formulas." For example, kindergarten and first-grade teachers have often been overheard to teach that "magnets attract metal" as a legitimate conclusion from an experiment in which they had provided magnets, and the only test objects were made of iron or steel or were nonmetals, thus completely overlooking such common, nonattracting metal objects as coins, aluminum foil, gold rings, and brass trinkets. The concept of ferrous metals does not come in until lower secondary school, but iron and steel belong somewhere in the upper elementary grades. There is no way to avoid the fact, however, that most children have more confidence in raising questions about folk science formulas than most teachers have in answering them. One "safe" and legitimate option is to chose topics that challenge children's interest and leave it to them. Lakatos' formula (1977), "The exception improves the rule," suggests a critical approach, whereas the folk formula, "the exception proves the rule," suggests a cover-up.

The folk science formulas given below have been overheard in classrooms, almost always without criticism. They represent a common, uncritical view and come from a wide variety of levels of sophistication. In some sense, some such folk science formulas may even provide a background for the conduct of scientific investigations. Because formulas like these are a part of our culture, we have all been exposed to some version of each of them. We may therefore object to some of them, for which we have a better version, and support others, which agree with what we were taught. For each one listed, I have added a preliminary criticism. Simply stating the criticisms seems to me to support and help these generalizations more often than to destroy them. I leave it to the reader to decide what kind of criticism it is—what the response should be. One caveat: Any context for these formulas has been omitted, to save space. Of course, when we recall and apply such a formula, we may have lost most of the original context or only recall contexts which are very limited, and thus lost most of the cognitive value of the original discovery which gave rise to the formula.

1. Plants breathe in carbon dioxide and breathe out oxygen. *Criticism:* Photosynthesis occurs in the presence of light, so it doesn't resemble breathing.
2. Action and reaction are equal and opposite. *Criticism:* What if I push someone over? My action is bigger than the other's reaction.
3. Gravity pulls things down and holds them to the earth. *Criticism:* That sounds so permanent. It can be overcome by other forces. Grass grows up. I can jump up, climb a ladder, and so on.
4. It's cold in the winter because the sun is farther away than it is in the summer. *Criticism:* In the Southern Hemisphere the seasons are opposite from ours. Is the sun a different distance from the people down there than it is from us? Why don't we write to children in Australia or New Zealand to find out what really happens down there?

5. There is no gravity in outer space. *Criticism:* Gravity holds the Earth in orbit around the sun, and all the other planets.

6. There is no gravity on the moon because it has no atmosphere. *Criticism:* The astronauts who went to the moon felt lighter up there, but they still fell back to the moon's surface when they jumped up.

7. Carbonation (acid) in drinks rots your teeth. *Criticism:* Sugar may be the chief cause of rotting teeth, as some second graders concluded after soaking some of their lost baby teeth in various solutions.

8. Every meal should be a balanced meal including vegetables animal protein, and starches. *Criticism:* The Inuit and vegetarians do not often eat such balanced meals.

9. The moon shines at night and the sun in the day. *Criticism:* The moon can be seen in the daytime.

10. Comets' tails always point away from the sun. *Criticism:* Sometimes they do not have a tail.

11. Blue is hotter than red. *Criticism:* This may apply to stars or to blue hot and red hot metals, but not to everyday objects at everyday temperatures.

12. Oxygen is a highly inflamable gas. *Criticism:* Oxygen is needed for the combustion of other gases so maybe it is not burned itself.

13. There are three states of matter: solids, liquids, and gases. *Criticism:* There are many states in between solid and liquid, silly putty, wet baking soda, tar, glass, gels, and so on. Plasmas, like the sun or in flourescent lights, are sometimes considered another state of matter.

14. Plants take their nourishment from the soil. *Criticism:* Nearly all of the parts of a plant turn into air and water when it is burned.

15. Blood flowing away from the heart is red and blood flowing to the heart is blue. *Criticism:* When I cut myself a little, the blood (going toward the lungs) is dark red, not blue.

16. Plants breath in carbon dioxide during the day and breathe in oxygen at night. *Criticism:* Plants do not have noses and mouths to inhale and exhale like animals.

17. Pivoted (equal-arm) balances for weighing things work like see-saws (or teeter-totters): *Criticism:* There is an important difference. A balance always comes to rest horizontal; a see-saw always comes to rest with one end down. You have to push a see-saw to make it go up and down.

18. Two batteries will make a flashlight bulb burn brighter than

one. *Criticism:* It depends on how they are connected, in parallel, in series, or in opposite directions.

18. Wind is the same thing as air in motion. *Criticism:* Updrafts, downdrafts, and air enclosed in a moving car are often not called wind (see the dictionary).

19. Open the windows in your house when a tornado approaches or the house may explode. *Criticism:* It may be more important to get to a safe place quickly.

I want children to remember important generalizations of science, but not to accept any formulas uncritically. Science in the elementary school can safely support the critical side of what scientists do in their research, not what they may do as teachers themselves. Remembering formulas is easier if one criticizes them than if one tries to remember them passively. Full acceptance or belief is not necessary. We would say, "Criticisms highlight the rule," based on the article cited earlier (Perry & Whitlock, 1955) that discusses the reading habits of many Harvard undergraduates. Believing or accepting something is not at all necessary to remembering it. From that and the common preconceptions teachers hold I infer that most teachers should not aim to have their pupils believing or accepting, just remembering, and that criticizing traditional formulas may be the best way for students to remember.

Most, if not all, science formulas within the official science curricula of schools have exceptions, qualifications, and various interpretations that are accessible to some children of elementary school age. Some are even indicated in texts but ignored as "too complex." Aside from social taboo there is no preventing a child challenging any formula in terms of what they pick up in school, from parents and other relatives, from television, and from news magazines. Because of the uncritical stance most teachers have learned to take in science, as children themselves, most of their pupils assume they should not look for criticisms or even mention those they could easily make. Once teachers realize that children are quite capable of raising reasonable arguments, however, they often become very happy to encourage such debate in their classrooms and, because the current scientific status of these formulas is not readily accesible to them, they even urge students to look elsewhere for additional critical ideas.

A first-grade teacher, who had been encouraging a lot of discussion of difficult story problems in math, called me to report in great excitement on a spontaneous science discussion in her class. It seems that she had made a statement that gravity was the force that held things on the earth. "That's not true," some argued, "grass grows up, people can jump up, climb ladders and steps. Airplanes and ballons, go up," and so, on and on the discussion went. The teacher simply happened to overhear this at one table and brought the question to the attention of the whole class. She had no idea that first-grade children could discuss science questions so well, she said. They argued back and forth, agreeing that gravity had an important role to play, but that it only seemed to hold things on the earth if there was nothing else sufficient to make them go up. This is exactly the sort of discussion I want to encourage, in which children can, by counter arguments, avoid any deleterious effects of science hubris, and enhance their recollections of what the teacher said. I wondered about the different meanings of the transitive verb "to hold" which scientists, science educators, teachers, and children might employ when they think of the statement the teacher made. My Webster's unabridged dictionary gives 11 current meanings, 5 of which are subdivided. None of them seem to fully justify what the teacher said, although one mentioned placing a barrier to limit motion and a Scottish colloquism alluded to suppressing motion. Several of the definitions were clearly supportive of the children's criticism, however.

Generally, the meanings of words develop with increasing sophistication, so adults, and especially scientists, may tacitly interpret some folk science formulas in a different way than children do. The exceptions evident to children can be managed by various adult devices not easily grasped by children. Indeed, at times a program of scientific research may focus on one formula, even demolishing its original meaning, without seeming to require its removal from the pool of formulas to which everyone is supposed to be introduced, for example, meteorological study of the vertical motion of air heated by contact with a hot spot on the earth. Such a mass of air, that is hotter than the surrounding air, but having the same absolute humidity, will be bouyed up by the greater pressure of the surrounding cooler air. In rising, however, it expands and cools (as meterologists say, "adiabatically," without heat being added or removed). As long as it remains warmer than the surrounding air, which is also cooler higher up, it continues to rise. If however, the surrounding air is as warm or warmer, the rise stops. If "hot air rises" means all that to you, you may be able to accept it. If not, you certainly might be critical of the formula, whether you are a teacher or a pupil. There's not much use in learning a formula you may never be able to justify with your own experience.

If one teacher invites children to criticize such formulas freely, the next few teachers that his or her pupils have, may not allow them to do so openly. The only hope for reform seems to be in the pupils' attitude toward such formulas. Here the question is, how long does it take to instill a critical attitude that can endure subsequent years of authoritarian teaching of uncriticized formulas? The teachers I have been working with suggest that although 1 year can do it for some students, 2 years are needed to really establish a critical attitude in the majority. A single teacher in an elementary school who finds it worthwhile to take this critical stance, might find it worthwhile to try to obtain a class containing two grade levels, and keep the same pupils for 2 years. Further research is needed.

There are a number of reasons why the critical, dialogic approach I am recommending should be helpful to future secondary school science students. First, it is only realistic to develop habits of sharing ideas and not to expect that one should be able to think of all the necessary ideas by oneself. Also, the attitude that teachers and texts will explain everything that needs to be known so that memorizing it all will guarantee success in every future demand is an all too common pathological result of science anxiety. Even when one wants to take pride in solving a particularly difficult problem in physics or chemistry by oneself, knowing to explore unusual ideas, and not just try all the obvious formulas, is a critical attitude that is too little developed by dependent but responsible students.

Second, learning a critical attitude is essential for developing and testing a consistent system of ideas. This cannot be managed so that most children in an elementary school class will have such a system by the end of the period or even by the end of the week. However, most children in most classes can develop a critical attitude in a relatively short time, and only the most insecure children may take a year. Elementary school is the most relaxed time for children to check their ideas for consistency and get ready for the pressures of secondary school where sometimes science classes cover a theory in a week.

Third, when consistent frames of theoretical ideas are finally presented in secondary school chemistry and physics, there will still be a strong need for flexibility. Just because the chemical bond chapter or the kinetic theory of gases chapter is being studied, does not mean that there is not a need to rethink some of the problems or experiments from an energy point of view. The more students do their own thinking about science the better.

ACKNOWLEDGMENTS

The writer is indebted to David Hawkins, Eleanor Duckworth, Keith Hanson, Bernadine Evans Stake, and Deborah Trumbull for their helpful comments on earlier drafts of this chapter but absolves them of all responsibility for its content.

REFERENCES

Apelman, M., Flexer, A. Carlson, R., & Hawkins, D. (1983). *A report of research on critical barriers to the learning and understanding of elementary science.* Boulder, CO: Mountainview Center, University of Colorado.

Driver, R. (1983). *The pupil as scientist?* Milton Keynes: The Open University Press.

Driver, R., Guesne, E., & Tiberghien, A. (1985). *Children's ideas in science.* Milton Keynes: The Open University Press.

Duckworth, E. (1983). Teachers as learners. *Archives de psychologie, 51,* 171–175.

Duckworth, E. (1987). *The having of wonderful ideas and other essays on teaching and learning.* New York: Teachers College Press.

Easley, J., & Sekita, K. (1989). *A follow-up study of peer-group dialogue.* Champaign, IL: CIRCE, University of Illinois at Urbana-Champaign.

Easley, J., & Zwoyer, R. (1975). Teaching by listening. *Contemporary Education, 47,* 19–25.

Ganot. (1873). *Elementary treatise on physics, experimenₜ ıl and applied* (6th ed.). New York: William Wood.

Grieb, A., & Easley, J. (1984). A primary school impediment to mathematical equity: Case studies in rule dependent socialization. In M. W. Steinkamp & M. L. Maehr (Eds.) *Recent advances in motivation: Vol. II. Women in science* (pp. 130–152). Greenwich, CT: JAI Press.

Hanson, K. (1984). Alternate theories in the classroom. In C. Anderson (Ed.), *Observing science classrooms: perspectives from research and practice* (pp. 39–52). Columbus: The Association for the Education of Teachers of Science.

Hanson, N. R. (1958). *Patterns of discovery: An inquiry into the conceptual foundations of science.* Cambridge: Cambridge University Press.

Harré, R. (1972). *Philosophies of science: An introductory survey.* Oxford: Oxford University Press.

Holton, G., & Roller, D. H. D. (1958). *Foundations of modern science.* Reading, MA: Addison-Wesley.

Jammer, M. (1957). *Concepts of force: A study in the foundations of dynamics.* Cambridge, MA: Harvard University Press.

Jammer, M. (1961). *Concepts of mass in classical and modern physics.* Cambridge, MA: Harvard University Press.

Kuhn, T. (1961). *The structure of scientific revolutions.* Chicago: The University of Chicago Press.

Lakatos, I. (1977). *Proofs and refutations: The logic of mathematical discovery.* Cambridge: Cambridge University Press.

Lakatos, I. (1979). *The methodology of research programmes.* Cambridge: Cambridge University Press.

Lemon, H.B., & Ference, M. (1946). *Analytical and experimental physics* (rev. ed.). Chicago: The University of Chicago Press.

Marshall, E. (1986). School reformers aim at creativity. *Science, 233,* 267–270.

Perry, W. G., Jr. (1970). *Forms of intellectual and ethical development in the college years: A scheme.* New York: Holt, Rinehart & Winston.

Perry, W. G., Jr., & Whitlock, C. P. (1954). A clinical rationale for a reading film. *Harvard Educational Review, 24,* 6–27.

Piaget, J. (1972). *La transmission des mouvements. Etudes d'épistémologie génétique* (Vol. 27). Paris: Presses Universitaires de France.

Piaget, J. (1980). *Les formes élémentaires de la dialectique.* Paris: Gallimard.

Piaget, J., & Garcia, R. (1974). *Understanding causality*, New York: W.W. Norton & Co.

Piaget, J., & Garcia, R. (1983). *Psychogenèse et histoire des sciences*. Paris: Flammarion.

Tipler, P. A. (1976). *Physics*. New York: Worth Publishers.

West, L. H. T., & Pines, A. L. (Eds.). (1985). *Cognitive structure and conceptual change*. Orlando: Academic Press.

Ziman, J. (1968). *Public knowledge: An essay concerning the public dimension of science*. Cambridge: Cambridge University Press.

4

Defining and Bridging the Gap

David Hawkins
University of Colorado

Some years ago Paolo Guidoni spoke about a loop in history by which some children grow to be teachers: Taught science little and poorly, they then teach little and poorly. Taken as the whole truth, this reminder is a counsel of despair. In matters affecting the teaching of science, most of us have been taught badly. John Dewey put it well: Science is too new, in our history, to have penetrated into the subsoil of mind. The subculture of science is still a restricted one and those who know it well, even at elementary levels, are a small minority. This is true especially among those who teach the young.

Guidoni's remark is only partly correct, I believe. But before we look for ways to qualify it, we should recognize some of its implications. The first of these has to do with scale, with numbers. The child population we consider is of the order of 15% of the total population, while that of its teachers, plus all those adults otherwise involved, is in the neighborhood of 1%. If we consider the teachers of children to be professional persons (as we should) their numbers exceed those of any other profession, very much so in poorer countries. And we must add that their average professional life, at least in the United States, is short—very short, for example, in comparison with that of medical doctors. In Lewis Carroll's *Through the Looking Glass* the Red Queen remarks that it is necessary to keep running in order even to stay in the same place. For progress to occur, the rate of improvement must exceed the rate of attrition.

Thus, for any major changes to be brought about in the cause of early science education there must be made, be evolved, some efforts of reform that are on a comparable scale. That evidently is large, and the question of resources is vital. Whose efforts, then, should we focus on? Ministries and departments of education may now, once more, decide they must give higher priority to science education; they will mostly, I fear, create commissions and committees, reports, then curriculum outlines and syllabi; then may come new textbooks and related print. The cost of these efforts will be a few cents per child. The results will be impersonal and mostly ineffective, so the cost per unit of significant effect will still be high. I do not rail against this, it is of the nature of most school bureaucracies. Their design is, with exceptions, for the maintenance of established ways of schooling, not for change. They can make change, although that may prove a struggle.

But there are other resources, more nearly on the scale required: those, in ministries or otherwise, who learn to stimulate the most powerful of influences for professional growth, the morale and commitment to further learning of the teachers themselves. But who can those persons be? And what resources can they offer? They are not a homogeneous group. They include good teachers of children who, in a collegial spirit, can help others—*if* they have time, opportunity, and moral support in doing so. They include many others of us from professional (or amateur) backgrounds, from the sciences and from educational research. But to bring about such liaisons, on a necessarily expanding scale, presupposes conditions—material conditions, and conditions of the spirit—which are now rare. Most teachers are overworked by demanding routines, by too-large classes, by a lack of needed professional support—and they often suffer from demoralization.

I have more to say about the needed changes. They are difficult and one may be pessimistic. But I have not yet dealt with the substance and spirit of what we would all agree to be good science education for children. If we had the opportunity to see it going on, at first hand, optimism would return. The ways in which children learn well should determine the ways in which we teach. The ways in which teachers learn well professionally, about *children's* learning, should determine the ways in which the growth of their own art and knowledge are given professional support. These remarks apply, of course, to all teaching, but the focus on science teaching offers special problems and opportunities.

In examining these problems and opportunities I suggest some reliable basis for optimism; to give, at least, one version of a consensus now emerging among these involved, and of which this book is one expression. This is not yet an optimism based on a high probability of change. That probability depends on robust political and institutional commitments that, I believe, do not yet exist. It is, rather, an optimism of possibilities. It is an optimism surely necessary to support the practical commitments we hope for (Easley, pp. 84–85).

As one of the contributors to this volume, therefore, I wish to express some of my own optimistic reflections on learning, inquiry, and teaching, with particular reference to the kinds of science we call *elementary*. As a philosopher and scientific amateur I have had a long-standing interest in these matters. Having in later years become involved with others in the practical work of helping teachers with their own learning and teaching of elementary science, I find that my earlier view of such matters has been quite radically affected. In particular, I have learned that any useful theoretical discussion must be interwoven with stories, case histories, and concrete examples. Otherwise, the meanings of the words we use can go astray. Let me then begin with one general theoretical statement, which I hope my examples illustrate and clarify. They are demonstrations of possibility.

THE UNIQUENESS OF SCIENCE

The uniqueness of science, as subject matter in the curriculum of childhood education, is in some ways related to the uniqueness of science in our history, of the ways it has grown and transformed the world. For an observer from almost any past period of history our world would appear strange indeed, almost incredible. It would be far stranger, said the historian Herbert Butterfield, than Nineveh and Tyre appear to us. Although familiar with some of its outer manifestations, we, ourselves, are disturbed and baffled by it, and very much of its inner scientific background escapes us. This can be true even of professional scientists, in their often intense specializations. "Scientific literacy" is always a matter of degree.

It is one of the conditions and consequences of this rapid historical growth that the scientific disciplines have built walls or dykes around themselves, maintaining rates of change beyond the capacity of the larger society to be part of or readily understand. As the knowledge of nature has grown it has undergone, as part of this growth, some major kinds of conceptual reorganization. These are changes that have not been easily achieved by the learned ones themselves, and are doubly difficult for those who live outside the walled cities of research. The walls are not impenetrable but they can be high. Although high schools and universities have come to provide much education in the sciences, the minority of students who have learned well have then mainly joined the ranks of the growing scientific professions, knowing they are wanted. The great majority of students, however, have gone their way, indifferent, forgetful, and often repelled by what they have supposedly been taught.

There are intriguing parallels between the history of the sciences and the patterns of successful science education, elementary or advanced. The examination of these parallels throws light, I believe, on the ways children learn well and, therefore, the ways in which we should learn to teach. As a kind of background for this examination, I refer here to one of the simplest and most illuminating descriptions of science that I know. It was written more than half a century ago by the great physicist Niels Bohr. In his introduction to a volume of essays concerning the then-new quantum physics, Bohr (1934) began as follows:

> The task of science is both to extend our experience and reduce it to order, and this task presents various aspects, inseparably connected with each other. Only by experience itself do we come to recognize those laws which grant us a comprehensive view of the diversity of phenomena. As our knowledge becomes wider we must always be prepared, therefore, to expect alterations in the points of view best suited for the ordering of our experience. (p. 1)

I love this brief and simple description because it suggests something important about the wide range of scientific activities and of the tensions, the connections, among them. At one pole, it is the aim and spirit of science to explore the worlds of nature, beyond what we routinely know or are taught for coping with them. A great deal of scientific discovery has come, and for children or adults can come, from a curiosity that focuses on rather everyday phenomena, but that does so with a refinement of discrimination that our normal working routines do not involve. This curiosity, this impulse to explore, to uncover phenomena previously overlooked or hidden, and to enjoy them, is minimized or overlooked in many discussions. It is over-looked because of a second phase of experience, which we more often call curiosity. This phase often follows the first but is dominated by *how* or *why* questions rather than the direct enjoyment of fresh experience. Yet without the first phase the second is unmotivated; without the second the process cannot be extended. In Bohr's language: we first seek to *extend* our experience; then to *reduce* it to order.

Two of us recently recalled a charming episode we were involved in, with a 6-year-old girl. By our arrangement she was playing with drops of colored water on a wax-paper surface, pushing the drops about with a pin. She separated large drops into two, merged two of different color, and generally was deeply engrossed as she spoke out her observations to us. And then, "I have *always* wondered why they hump up like that!" No doubt there was previous casual experience of that "humping" of the liquid surface, now recalled. She was no stranger to water play. But this time it was sharply in focus and the why question, the "always wondered," was more for esthetic delight than as any sort of footnote to a 6-year-old's autobiography. Because no explanations were in fact forthcoming, or available, the first phase of curiosity stood out. We could indeed have gone on, as we have on other occasions, to other phenomena involving liquid-surface energies, such as the dimples on the pond-surface made by the feet of water bugs, or the melting of ice cubes floating in salad oil. Both children and adults can see that there is kinship among such phenomena, which cluster together in their thinking by some sense of analogy among them. In Bohr's language: When we extend our experience in such ways we are already beginning to reduce it to order, even at a stage when the talk of "surface energy" would be useless and pretentious verbiage, the sort of verbiage bad textbooks for children sometimes engage in. At an honest level of inquiry we have heard children, and adults, finally announce that such surfaces are both "stretchy" and somehow "dry." This declaration does not come soon, nor without hesitation. As every one knows, water is *wet!* This is common sense! But "as our knowledge becomes wider we must always be prepared . . . to expect alterations in the points of view best suited for the ordering of our experience" (Bohr, 1934, p. 1). The "dry" stretchy surface of water is delicate, and even the water bug's oily feet must not stretch it too far; on pain of drowning. It is a phenomenon of a more minute scale in nature than we great beings will easily notice, until we begin deliberately to "extend our experience" downward in the scale of sizes. As we do, there arises the challenge to unify our previously established common sense with what has newly been found. Pursued in depth, the investigation of such surface phenomena will lead even farther down in the scale of sizes to the ionic bonds of water molecules, for which our young children and scientifically naive adults are not yet quite prepared. Indeed the many phenomena of surface chemistry are today still up for detailed investigation. Yet the untutored ones have taken a step, of enlarging their experience and beginning to unify it; and there are many other related steps accessible to them. This is only one small example (e.g., Hawkins, 1975) of ways the unity of nature begins to be reflected in the unity of understanding. And that, rather than the flat explanations of the elementary school textbooks (often wrong or misleading) is science: In the poet's language, it is one way "to see the world in a grain of sand"—or a drop of water.

ARISTOTLE AND GALILEO

In the history of science there are abundant examples of the twofold task Bohr spoke of. Some of these, also, have recently come under investigation as examples of difficulty in the present-day teaching of elementary science. They give substance to the parallels between original discovery and student learning. I describe one of these that, I believe, leads to further steps in the discussion of learning and teaching. It also happens to be one that is of great historical importance in the growth of physics, invoking the names of Aristotle, Galileo, and Newton.

Aristotle, the greatest of the ancient Greek philosopher–scientists, attempted to develop a general theory around the topic of motion. This interest, this commitment to find some general theory, illustrates the second part of Bohr's description of science, the search for a unifying point of view, from which many diverse phenomena can be understood. In Aristotle's time the many forms of motion that common sense might recognize had been extended to include motions on a scale far vaster than ever before conceived. The Greek astronomers had already, by that time, "reduced to order" the vast complex of motions in the heavens, of the stars and planets, moon and sun. Theirs was a geometrical model with a tiny Earth in the center, surrounded by very many transparent spheres that rotated around it. The outermost of these carried myriad lights, the fixed stars that we see wheeling overhead at night. The innermost carried the Moon, and defined its orbit (two or three were actually needed for that, to account for departures from strictly circular motion). In between were many spheres to mimic the motions of the sun and other planets.

This whole story, developed by the Greeks from the astronomical records of Mesopotamia and Egypt, has been one of the inspirations for much of modern science; it is our first historical example of a major scientific development, a way station, at least, on the road to present-day cosmological knowledge. Aristotle loved this story, we know it mainly from his writings. But it was a challenge to his understanding, and to common sense ideas of motion.

Some kinds of motion, Aristotle knew, could be maintained only with a push or a pull from some external agent. You have to push the cart to keep it going, its "natural state" is at rest. Other kinds of motion seem to require no such agent, things move of their own accord: the rock falls into the well, the smoke rises away from the center. In the heavens, on the contrary, everything appears to be self-moving in the circumferences of great astronomical circles. The things of the earth are made of one kind of matter, said Aristotle, while those of the heavens moving neither up nor down, must be of quite another; they require no external force to keep them going.

In the late Middle Ages some followers of Aristotle faced up to a difficulty. If lateral motion here below requires something pushing to maintain it, what of the arrow, which continues its flight *after* it has left the bowstring? Well, it was suggested, the bow has communicated a push from the string in the arrow's nock, but has also produced an invisible "impetus" that stays with the arrow for a time, impelling it along but finally used up; whereupon the arrow falls straight down, its "natural" motion.

I tell this tale at some length because the central belief it embodies is still very much alive and well in our own time, despite endless pronouncements, from tests and lectures, of its falsity. If Aristotle had had access to a "hockey puck" made of carbon dioxide ice and a large flat table surface of glass, he could have discovered that an object moving horizontally *will* continue that motion *until* it is acted upon by some external force. The puck is almost as self-moving as are the heavenly bodies. The cart or the arrow would maintain their motion also if no forces acted to slow them down, the forces we call *friction*. Galileo announced this proposition against the Aristotelians. External forces do not act to maintain motion, but only to change it; on Earth or in the heavens the laws are the same. Formulated with quantitative precision this is the essence of Newton's first two laws of motion, which unified the ideas of terrestrial and celestial motion.

Yet there is something about this apparently simple idea that unfits it to enter many minds easily or, if it enters, to stay there for long. The research referred to has amply documented the fact that students in first-year courses of physics—high school or university—continue to suppose that the maintenance of a constant velocity requires a constant applied force (Minstrel, 1984). They may have "done the problems" at the end of each chapter, may even have received a fair grade for their work. Yet once out of that classroom context they often revert to some ingrained common sense. The numbers of students, the proportions who demonstrate this behavior, are not small. It is as though the mind's immune system were rejecting some alien tissue graft.

The research in question is essentially diagnostic and does not adequately point the way to any significant revision, of teaching style or content, except perhaps by implication. I return to this topic in a later section, in which I do propose such revision. To do that, however,

I wish first to extend this theoretical discussion, referring again to the quotation from Niels Bohr. If we have indeed extended our experience and sought out new points of view for organizing it, there remains a further phase of the process that his statement does not make explicit. The story of force and motion serves well to suggest the nature of this phase. It has to do with a necessary reconciliation between new points of view, suggested in the widening of experience, and older points of view, congenial and well established on the basis of earlier experience. As in the case of the "dryness" of water surfaces, or of Galileo's law of inertial motion and the whole system of Newtonian mechanics, the new and the old must be tested against each other and then somehow reconciled. In the aftermath of the great modern scientific triumph, however, Aristotle was almost always convicted, by unscholarly scientific commentators, of profound error. His medieval followers, then, were condemned as guilty of slavish and totally unscientific discipleship, of reliance on authority rather than clear evidence.

Such historical judgments are, of course, partly correct, but they are also arrogant. As his dialogues clearly show, Galileo had to dig through layers of accumulated belief and argument before the basic law of inertia could be established; it was not easy. Even he did not formulate it with full generality. A substantial reason for the difficulty of this achievement lies in the fact that Aristotle, his medieval followers, and vast numbers of present-day students and their elders are quite right in these ways of thought they hold to. Error arises when these ways of thought are extended beyond the range of experience from which they have been derived. Moreover, this "erroneous" way of thought has long been incorporated within Newtonian physics. Aristotle's arguments, so far as they are valid, have been reformulated and refined as the theory of motion in a resisting medium. What once was accepted theory was not simply lost or discarded. It now finds a place within a more ample scheme in which forces of resistance are matched by forces of propulsion. When the physicist has to push his car to the nearest filling station he thinks just as Aristotle did. But he can also translate these thoughts immediately into a framework profoundly different from Aristotle's. Instead of supposing that the motion itself requires a force to maintain it, he knows that the motion will continue if his pushing just cancels other forces, forces that are very real but that have somehow not always entered the equations of common sense; in this case, the friction forces of pavement and wheels.

I have discussed this example of the understanding of inertial motion at some length because it offers, I believe, a good starting point for some general remarks related to our traditional teaching practices in

the sciences. These seem to be based on a different sort of epistemological belief than that which my examples clearly suggest. This belief
is that, prior to our teaching, our students' minds are simply empty of
the enlightening knowledge we transmit to them. Having helped them
fill some empty mental storage places, we have no way of understanding how or why this content is lost for later and wider use. We
then worry that our exposition was inadequate, or that the students
were inattentive, or lacking in scientific intelligence; were the ideas
somehow too difficult?

Our new way of thinking, now pretty amply confirmed by research,
assumes that those "empty storage places" of the students' minds are
not empty at all; they are already full, and so must somehow be
enlarged. Our teachings are held in some transient memory but they are
not embedded in their minds for further use and development. In John
Dewey's language they are accepted but not controlled, and so are
finally lost. In the language of Piaget there is a failure in the unitary
process that he called "assimilation," "accommodation," "equilibration." Here, however, I return to the language of Bohr, who thought
deeply on such matters.

THE PRINCIPLE OF CORRESPONDENCE

Elsewhere in the writing I have referred to Bohr's (1934) formulation—
for the purposes of research—of what he called the "Principle of
Correspondence." Having in some ways extended our experience, and
finding that it is not entirely consonant with previous ways of understanding, we seek some new point of view from which we can find
order in it. But we do not first find the new order, and only then seek
to reconcile it with previous habits of thought. That separation appears
only in hindsight. On the contrary the order-seeking process must from
the beginning involve some loyalty to earlier ways of thought, ways
known already to have some genuine validity but standing now in need
of qualifications that do not simply "overthrow" them. The notion of
"scientific revolution," of the shift from one "paradigm" to another,
sometimes thought of as though everything previously known were
thrown out, is profoundly misleading.

Bohr's own research in atomic physics, continued by others whom
he influenced profoundly, involved such a re-examination of previous
physical theory. A major part of this "classical physics" survived
intact and gave form, gave guidance, to the reformulation that came to
be known as quantum physics. It is only after this new physical theory
had been built and showed its power that one could treat it as though

it simply stood opposed to older ideas. High school physics teachers will be amused at the language of Bohr, who referred to the older ideas of classical physics that they still must teach, as "common sense." But for Bohr and his associates it was. Common sense exists at all levels of scientific sophistication, it refers simply to ideas that at any level have become completely habitual.

When we study the history of science we find that this loyalty to older ways of thought, however it may have to have been qualified in developing the new, has been an indispensable guide. And it is so, I argue, for that of science teaching. Here the history involved is that of the student's own understanding, brought back to consciousness.

A part of their role of authority is that teachers understand not only the subject matter they teach, but also apply themselves to the art of helping students explicate their own ways of thinking, their "alternate conceptions" (Driver et al., 1985) and the "critical barriers" (Apelman et al., 1985) that if not understood may generate failure; and that if understood, may bring successes. Learning in this way from their students, teachers also broaden their own understanding. Some of these naive alternatives, brought out and examined, may prove to have unexpected merit; sometimes for the topic at hand, sometimes for other topics they may suggest. (Our own work is summarized in Apelman, Colton, Flexer, & Hawkins, 1981.) For a recent critical review, see Hills (1989). An undeniable merit is that when students become conscious of their own ways of thinking they are—only then—able to engage in reconstructing them.

Lacking this sense of openness, of playfulness with ideas, examples of which are reported in chapter 2, we are easy victims of authoritarian pronouncements quite alien to the spirit of science. Indeed, we always live on the threshhold of phenomena that are accessible to common experience but still wide open to investigation. I give another example that philosophers have long battled over, and in which dogmatic exposition can lead us sadly astray.

A Puzzle From Optics

The reconstruction of our ways of thinking about motion is difficult for many, it seems to go against the grain of some deeply channeled intuition. But the final resolution is well-known, extended, and summarized by Newton's laws. There are other topics of elementary science, however, about which "naive" ways of thinking may touch the boundaries of still-unresolved questions of scientific research. "Alternate" ways of thinking about phenomena, different that is from received scientific ideas, may be condemned as false by dogmatic teaching, when in fact they may lead in interesting and important directions, of which we ourselves have not previously been aware. Sometimes these may in the end prove useless. Sometimes they prove to be novel ways of reaching familiar conclusions, or topics of great interest that lie to one side of the textbook track. As teachers, we will not know how to deal with such suggestions or questions unless we respect them and follow their implications.

I take an example from the history and present-day teaching of geometrical optics. This is a topic behind which there is a long tradition of research and speculation. In modern times we have separated this ancient subject matter into two quite distinct areas of investigation. One of these is the geometry and physics of light, more generally of electromagnetic radiation. The other is that of vision, which we place under the heading of epistemology or of neurobiology. For native common sense, however, and for all but relatively recent science, they are inseparably connected. How is it that our eyes perceive things at a distance, or see themselves in a mirror? There are many ancient investigations, from the Greeks and from the medieval Arabic thinkers; and they involve two quite different common sense ideas (see Ronchi, V., 1957). One is that of a ray *from* the eye that goes *out* to the object of vision, to scan or "feel" its surface, so to speak, and thus to construct a copy, an image. The other is that the object itself somehow sends its form or image *to* the eye. Plato adopted both points of view. The Greek Epicureans said that the image came *to* the eye. The Arabs drew the arrows of vision *from* the eye. In fact what we call geometrical optics accords equally well with either way of thinking. Both the children and the teachers we have worked with have shown this same ambivalence, using now the one representation, now the other, and sometimes both. This seems to depend on the specific phenomena which are being observed or discussed. Glanced at quickly, the sun shines *in* our eyes, as does the bright lamp or torch. Whereas the tree or the moon we see *out there* at some distance. In the one case, the eye is thought of as a receptacle of light coming into it. In the other it is the instrument of a vision that reaches out to touch or scan the surface of some distant object (cf. Henriques, pp. 147–148).

It was Johannes Kepler, working just before the time of Galileo, who first was able to show that our seeing of external objects involves the transmission of light from those objects through the eye lens to form an image on the sensitive tissue of the retina. In the aftermath of this discovery, it is all too easy to conclude that we do not really see external objects but only our own retinal images—and they are upside down! Why then don't we see the world that way, inverted? Many textbooks, many teachers of elementary optics or of philosophy, and so also many students, have accepted this conclusion as a kind of dogma, "scientific truth", and the puzzle it implies. So the Epicurean view is the scientific one, they believe, and that of the Arabs is wrong: nothing goes *out* from the eye! Yet oddly enough the Arab view is not gone; it comes creeping back. In interviews with many students and some adults I have heard much language that conveys something like the following representation: The retina (two eyes of course, but one will do) is a kind of television screen on which images are formed by light from external sources. This screen is viewed from within a kind of inner viewing room by a little viewer sitting there; and that viewer's vision reaches *out* to its object on the screen. So both representations have now come back into the account! But, of course, the same way of thinking, improperly called "scientific," will now lead to a new trouble. The mental viewing room, though, not a literal "hole in the head" is still something like it, nerve-circuitry that transmits signals from and to the "center." The little viewer back there now has the original problem all over again. He or she is not directly aware of the objects on the screen, but only receives signals from them, only sees images of the "inner eye." And so on!

In our research with teachers this particular confusion caused no trouble at first. Mature and intelligent persons who wished to remedy their ignorance of science, they seem to have had no place in their thinking for even the rudiments of Kepler's kind of optics as a source of understanding or of confusion. I discuss our work together later on, as illustrating the kind and level of scientific experience that teachers of the young can profit by. But more needs to be said first about Bohr's Principal of Correspondence. I wish to call attention to it as a rule which is relevant at all levels of learning and teaching. I also, as I have said, use the term *common sense* as a label for any mode of understanding, however naive or learned, which has gained acceptance and fluency in the mind of a child, a scientist, or a teacher. Let me give Bohr's principle a different name, then, one more suited to present purposes: the *Principle of the Conservation of Common Sense* (Vicentini, 1980). I take it in a somewhat more general sense than Bohr needed to. It implies not only an essential need for accommodation between the old and the new. It also implies that where this accommodation fails, the new ways of thought, which have been transiently learned, are easily lost, in a year or in 10. Or at best the new will get isolated, in some separate compartment of the mind. As between the common human culture and the newer culture of science, isolated from each other, the old ways of thought will thus often prevail, even in our world so much transformed by science.

In making use of parallels between the history of scientific discovery and the present-day learning of science I intend no dogma, but only use the idea as a guide. The work I discuss has been done mainly in connection with science education for adults, specifically for teachers of the young. In that connection we seem to find, repeatedly and in many contexts, that the thought habits of present-day adults (those who are scientifically naive) are remarkably close to those revealed in the ancient literature. In view of the many radical changes in the daily life, in the very world of present-day adults, as compared to the ancients, this seems particularly striking. I do not wish to develop the evidence for this conclusion here, or its implications, beyond the suggestion that there is some remarkable stability in these aspects of culture, of native common sense, across long intervals of time.

In such connections one thinks of course of Piaget's rather grandly conceived genetic epistemology. Piaget (1970) said, perhaps half-jokingly, that in view of the parallelism between history and individual development, his major reason for studying children was to throw light on history. This is much the same spirit as that of the evolutionist of today who goes to the laboratory of molecular genetics in order to find evidence concerning the ancient past of life on earth. In view of what recent research has found, however, it does not seem even plausible to suppose that children's development could parallel that of the history of science, and yet produce adults whose common sense was so little changed from ancient times. As Matilde Vicentini (1980) has re-marked, Piaget did not study adults. In honoring his name by doing so, we are led to a rather different view of genetic epistemology. Although surely the mind structures of today must differ in many ways from those of the ancients, it would appear that in the logical schemes they hold relevant to scientific understanding, many scientifically naive adults of today are hardly different from those of many generations past—accommodated superficially to new phenomena and language, but not changed. Although everyone knows that the astronauts float "weightless" above the earth and even, "float" at a fixed point above the equator, the attempt of many of us to conceptualize this informa-tion, to "reduce it to order," has a strong resemblance to medieval conceptions of the flight of angels. The thought patterns of many children, under the prevailing conditions of schooling and television, will mature not to approximate some Piagentian ideal, but still, rather, to those of Aristotle.

In a more generous interpretation, Piaget's genetic epistemology does not refer to our own adult world. It refers rather to a kind of parallel between the history of scientific development and the ways in which some more fortunate children of today can recapitualate the conceptual struggles and conjectures that mark the earlier history. And this may also be true of many teachers of today, as they struggle to learn. I return to this matter later.

SCIENCE FOR THOSE WHO HAVE AVOIDED IT

The Guidoni loop mentioned earlier is only a first approximation, and I promised to qualify it. The loop is real but the description of it needs revision. The failure of scientific knowledge and understanding among many teachers is a major part of the situation we face, but not all of it. Another is a traditional style of teaching to which most of our schools have been deeply committed, and still are. This style of teaching, even if indulged in by teachers who are themselves well educated in science, will characteristically reach only those children who need it least, and who can learn for themselves, in any case. A different style of teaching can be far more effective, even if this is carried on by teachers who are not very well educated scientifically. They can carry on, if bold enough, both for themselves and for their children. I speak mainly of a range of subject matters appropriate to the work and learning of elementary school teachers. That is where much of my own major experience lies, and with subjects that make the smallest demands on teachers' previous "formal" education, yet have some genuine mind-opening powers.

I have also been involved at a beginning level of university science teaching, dealing mainly with first- and second-year students, some of whom were future teachers. These usually had avoided even the most superficial acquaintance with the sciences. I myself had begun quite differently, with a childhood addiction to astronomy, to chemistry, to play with electricity and to home-made radios, to rocks and minerals, and so forth. This play was wholly unrelated to any schooling. Becoming later a student of philosophy, mainly concerned with the philosophy of science, I was still largely an amateur, self-taught in the sciences. I therefore had ample opportunity, later on, to learn along with my students. I very soon discovered that lecturing and patient "explanations" did little to help them either to get excited about the wonders of nature, or to untie the conceptual knots that our subject seemed to create. This forced me to a more careful analysis of their difficulties, often so "elementary" that I myself had no memory of ever having felt them. In the course I taught I managed, at least, to avoid the standard and dismal separation between "lecture" and "laboratory." We were together for 6 or 8 hours a week in which I lectured (in retrospect too much!), and we engaged in improvised demonstrations, or lab experiments; or just discussed and played. We took field trips for geology, but also for geometry and astronomy. Sitting on the eastern edge of the Rocky Mountains, Boulder has a billion years of geological history accessible to the discerning eye. Stationed with stop watches at different elevations of a nearby mountain, we could measure the diameter of the earth by timing the sunrise or moonrise.

In all of these endeavours I was trying to depart from the standard prescriptions of science teaching. These had already failed my students! But I departed from those prescriptions too little, or so I now believe. My small successes, of course, stand out in memory. I describe one of these here. It relates to Aristotle and Galileo on motion. More importantly, it was for me a clear example of the use, in teaching, of something like Bohr's Principle of Correspondence: of the value of first confronting students with phenomena for which their common sense ideas and habits of thought *were* already well suited, calling these ideas clearly to mind in the process, even strengthening them. In this way, I believed, what has been merely habitual can become consciously controlled, and *only* then intelligently related to new ranges of phenomena, showing how these older ideas can be qualified without being proven simply wrong.

Our course began with a study of mechanics and, from this, of Newton's "reduction to order" of the motions of planets in the solar system. After a few years' experience I had realized that even the first step, Galileo's "simple" law of inertia, *was* unintelligible to many students. So I began a new year—always hopeful—with the topic of motion in a quite tangible medium. We therefore started with "floating and sinking," and managed the conclusion that only objects denser than water would sink; if less dense they would rise. This involved the concept of density, a *pons asinorum* for many; it took some time. We investigated weighted balls, corks, boats of copper foil, and so on. We then went on to investigate the speed at which balls of different density would rise or sink. These were small weighted plastic balls in water, oil, sugar solutions, and also balloons falling or rising in air. The initial challenge had been a simple one: If clouds are made of tiny droplets of *liquid* water, why don't they fall like the big raindrops? From our experiments we evolved a formula (although the students groaned even at the simple algebra), which covered all the variables that seemed relevant: density difference, surface area of the spheres, and something (viscosity) which we called "stickiness." *All* of this was consistent with Aristotle on motion, and even improved on him. From the formula we evolved we got our answer about the cloud droplets: They *do* fall. But only very slowly! With a bit of apparatus we even timed the fall of such tiny droplets, confirming our predictions.

It was 2 weeks of hard work. The success became evident, however, with the introduction of a new topic. I skipped beyond Galileo's law of inertia and went on to a topic that usually comes later in the textbook, his law of falling bodies. Our leading question was: What would our formula tell us about the speed of a rock falling from a nearby balcony? The formula gave a very high velocity indeed, far greater than our clocking showed it to be.

In all our other measurements the speed of the object through liquid or air was constant, except for the *very* brief moment after it was released and speeded up to its terminal velocity. This period of acceleration had been so brief as to go unnoticed. With the rock from the balcony, on the other hand, there was almost constant acceleration from rest, as Galileo had long since concluded. If the rock had been dropped from a high-up balloon, the acceleration would indeed have begun to decrease until its terminal velocity was reached, at a speed (hundreds of feet per second) which our formula *could* indeed rather accurately predict. It was just a formula for terminal velocity in a resisting medium, *not* a general law of motion.

I recall some of the discussion. We did a sort of thought experiment with our now-questionable formula, knowing that it made good sense and summarized many measurements quite well; but not yet appreciating its limitation. The thought experiment was to consider what it said about motion in a medium that offered *no* resistance, in which the measure of "stickiness" or viscosity was zero. "The formula doesn't make any sense, then," I was primly told, "you can't divide by zero!" "So the stickiness *can't* be zero, just very small—always." But another disagreed. "Why can't you divide by zero? That just means the speed would be infinite!" Both were, I realized, still close to Aristotle. We had a vacuum pump and did the old demonstration of the coin and feather dropping together in the vacuum. So it was, finally, that *acceleration* came sharply into focus, and we got on to Galileo and Newton. There were other troubles along the way, of course. The generality of an idea does not come upon us, full-grown. But the first hurdle was passed, and we seemed to know that others could be.

I cannot recall all my thinking at the time, but in retrospect I believe that these Stokes' law experiments we did had served to sharpen, to quantify and so dignify a common sense preconception *before* getting on to a more ample conceptual scheme. The common sense, Aristotelian scheme, could only then be challenged, reflected upon, and yet still find its place. In some measure, at least, common sense had been conserved, and even been seen to support the newer point of view rather than contradict it.

Many of my experiences in those years led me to the conclusion that my "scientifically illiterate" students had somehow gotten off of any fruitful learning track in their earlier years, and that repeated failure (in earlier schooling) had deeply underscored their difficulties. I was powerfully supported in this conclusion by my wife, Frances Hawkins, a professional teacher of young children, who knows only too well the predominant conditions of early failure in our schools.

DESIGN OF MATERIALS—A FIRST STEP

After 15 years of such experience I was fortunate to find a position in a national elementary school science project (The Elementary Science Study, ESS), and I there had the opportunity to observe and reflect upon the school-based origins of early failure, my students' and my own. In that project we could not find experienced teachers of the young to educate us about the optimal conditions of early science learning, and our work often suffered from this defect. We had, I think, two saving virtues. One was a commitment to the belief that children's learning of science could best come through their own investigative activities, when properly encouraged and supported. The first part teachers should play, we believed, was to *invest* the chosen subject matter. In Latin the word "invest" meant literally to clothe. In a more general metaphoric sense it means to clothe with charm and entice-ment, with a sense of importance. Good teachers, even those who are scientifically naive themselves, can do that, can attract and support children's investigative curiosity. In doing so they can provide re-sources and a supportive ambiance, can question and summarize, and then—with help—extend what has been learned to further topics. We designed and wrote for teachers in that spirit.

Our other virtue was that any material we prepared as a guide for teachers—a teaching unit, with guidebook and lab equipment—was evolved through our own repeated personal experience in work with children. Accompanied by a colleague who acted as observer and critic, we became visiting teachers in borrowed classrooms. With good, simple lab equipment, and with such support, children will seldom let you fail. Still, we often had our own preconceptions shaken, about science and about children.

In our second year of that project, I was invited to visit the Nuffield Junior Science Project in England, and there saw a quite different style of development. The staff of that project worked always *with* teachers, acting as co-teachers, as frequent visitors, to classrooms. They thus provided material, intellectual and moral support. We, on the other hand, had worked much less in this collegial relationship with teachers. As a result of this visit to England, I realized that most teachers needed far more help than we had offered. In preparing our kits of apparatus and materials, along with guide books, we were hoping for large-scale national distribution. Very often, as we increasingly learned, these fell on barren ground. I remembered the Larousse motto, *Je sème a tout vent*. The dandelion makes many seeds, but only a few take root and flourish. The elephant makes very few. But with a great investment of gestation and nurture, most of the young survive. Which way is best? In matters affecting educational change, surely, some combination is best. In the courses we and others gave, our teachers, like children, often became excited by the fresh learning of scientific matters which came from their own investigations and discussions. But we were naive to expect that this experience of learning through their own investigation would of itself empower them to provide, in the same style, for their children's learning.

The Help Teachers Need

It was from these observations and reflections that Frances Hawkins and I redirected our efforts. What we had seen in England and on a later year-long visit had become part of, was a new–old style of classroom work that de-coupled children from constant didactic efforts, allowing them to work through most of a day as individuals or in small groups (the classes were then very large, 35–40), their teacher circulating among them. This work was mediated by a ready supply of inexpensive materials for model construction, for stitchery, for drawing and painting and mapping, for the study of plant growth and small animal nurture and behavior, for the study of light and color, for measurement and geometry, for simple mechanics, for reading and writing. Occasional field trips brought collections to arrange and exhibit. More importantly, these trips could provide fresh challenges for further work, for reading, writing, for painting. There were children's books for reference and enjoyment; not many "schoolbooks." Local archaeology and history sometimes set the stage, and again books were important but secondary. We recall tape recordings of the reminiscences of elder citizens, pleased and stimulated by children's historical curiosity. Old buildings could be studied, even castles, town and church records could be examined. Educational writers have often urged the "integration" of subject matter in the elementary school. This is what we often observed, but we decided to call it, instead, nondisintegration. When subjects had not first been torn apart, no "integration" was needed.

Not all the classes we observed were uniformly of this quality, but most had some of it and most teachers were committed to it in some measure. Their work was hard and underpaid, but they were learning, and enjoyed the recognition of success. How had such changes come about? They had evolved over time, mainly since World War II but with a background from earlier times, from the traditions of Froebel, of John Dewey and English pioneers of "progressive education." They were still evolving. This evolution, which became widespread in the infant schools (ages 5–7) and only somewhat less in the junior schools (ages 7–11), was mediated by a rather close-woven network of professional support for the teachers: national inspectors, local inspectors and advisors, teachers-college faculties, teachers' centers, all were involved in the spread of this style of school program. It was not a plan superimposed from above; neither was it something rising wholly from the grass roots. There were holiday courses that saw teachers working with materials that had been evolved in other classrooms, and in discussing the reduction to practice of ideas to help plan and organize the "integrated day." Much of this professional support came also through a pattern of classroom visits, when teachers and their advisors could work together in a collegial relation. Headmasters and headmistresses were often selected for their own practical knowledge and teaching skills, and could be an important part of this support system. One had a clear demonstration of the fact that the evolution came not from the top, downward, nor from the bottom upward, but in both ways meeting; there were inventive teachers and thoughtful advisers, each adding to the repertoires and insights of the others.

This development we had the chance to study was by no means uniform; it was much more conspicuous in some local authorities than others. It was ample enough, in some places, guided by doughty advisors, to show substantial improvements even in the standard maths and reading scores of the then-universal national eleven-plus examinations. Evolution is always, in principal, uneven. Hard times in England later ushered in a government with a zeal for budget cutting and a regressive view of early education. The evolution we enjoyed observing has thus been inhibited and sometimes reversed in its course; it still persists, however, and stands as an ample demonstration. We know other places, in other countries including our own, where such demonstrations have succeeded, although none on the same scale. In the United States they are still few and far between. The redirection of our work that came after these visits was our own fresh effort, in the United States, to provide for teachers some measures of professional support that could begin to parallel those we had found in England and Wales.

At the beginning of this chapter I spoke about the scale of significant improvement in science education, about the serious involvement in that process of very large numbers of persons—of teachers themselves—contributing their talents to it. This clearly is necessary, although not sufficient. Others need to be involved in the several ways in which teachers' efforts must be encouraged and supported. The right metaphor is indeed not "top-down" and not "bottom-up," but both together. The best idea would be that of collegiality, in which the usual implications of "top" and "bottom" are quite blurred.

In the times of the ESS curriculum project, however, we sometimes heard a boast from others involved in such curriculum reform efforts: They would, they said, produce teaching materials of such good quality that these would be "teacher proof." Or in a milder but no less arrogant version, that they would also provide courses for teachers that would "retread" them, like worn-out tires. Such phrases only exaggerated certain beliefs that were too prevalent among university-based folk, "subject matter specialists." Some of us were not guilty of such arrogance. But we failed, as I have said, to understand fully the kinds of support that good teachers would ask for and all would need. Our own guidebooks were as nondirective as we could make them, pointing out choices for teachers and children where we had the wit to do so, supporting an avoidance of daily "lesson plans," suggesting informal and diversified classroom organization. But these benign commitments were not enough.

The central concern of that period had been to improve early science education by providing curriculum materials designed to be administered by teachers but not aimed primarily toward their own learning *as* teachers, as teachers who would then be competent to teach well because they had in turn been well taught. In the hands of some teachers, I believe, our materials were indeed well used; these had added to teachers' own repertoires, not subtracted from their professional initiative. But for many others the intent and the content were inaccessible; our materials were translated into didactic lesson plans or, often enough, simply gathered dust in the school's storehouse.

The whole U.S. enterprise of that time resembled a kind of "invasion from Mars," the invaders being academic scientists who knew little about teaching the young but who saw a genuine need for reform and devoted themselves to it with enthusiasm; and who often optimistically misjudged the education of teachers, the bureaucratic and cultural ambiance of our schools. We misjudged the readiness of most teachers to adopt a style of teaching that they poorly understood and that, so far as they did understand it, involved threatening deviations from standard practices. We provided no paper-and-pencil tests of the sort that would accompany a standard curriculum called "Science," different children's work would seemingly diverge along different paths; their learning would require observation and judgment rather than those "objective" test scores, a paragraph rather than a letter or number grade. But above all, many of these teachers were inexperienced in the art of investment, of enticing and supporting children's own investigative curiosity and of providing for it beyond the immediate lesson. Being inexperienced, they were often mistrustful that their children could display the imagination and resourcefulness that our sorts of materials—at their best—could help evoke. Such teachers often expressed their misgivings in a more synoptic form, a concern for "discipline." If children were allowed to work at their own apparatus, to move about freely, were encouraged to discuss matters with others, out from under any immediate control, then there would be noisy and troublesome behavior. Such teachers' experience had not allowed them to learn just the opposite, that discipline problems arise mainly from confinement, silence—and boredom.

Such at least is my present diagnosis. At the time we either optimistically overlooked such matters or, when we faced them, felt powerless to deal with them. In our most insightful discussions we said that if teachers could learn to overcome these threats and experience the successes that were possible, then the same style of work could spread into other parts of the curriculum; a consummation devoutly to be desired.

A Center for Teachers

With such reflections and with the English experience in our background, and the knowledge of earlier American experience from the same traditions, we set out to create a local advisory center for teachers. This was in the nature of an experiment, one that would offer intensive professional support for teachers who sought it or would learn to seek it. If successful, it could demonstrate a widely prevalent need, and a way of meeting it. In this effort we were not alone, there were a few others in different parts of this large country, begun at about the same time and with some similar perception of need. Our center was located on the edge of the University campus, easily accessible to teachers. We welcomed them first as casual visitors—to talk, to look at work in progress, to inquire about our courses. Some then came regularly, and of these some asked us to work in their classrooms. Sometimes these visits were to help them initiate a new activity, which might be craft work, or mathematics in the concrete mode, or a new kind of field trip.

Sometimes it was for help with a particular child, sometimes just for conversation and discussion of their work.

I believe that our work differed from that of other centers in the emphasis we gave to teacher's own fresh encounters with subject matter. In a famous passage A.N. Whitehead (1949) spoke of a cycle of phases in the process of educationally important learning. These phases, he said, are those of romance, then detail, then generalization. In our teachers' own educational background the romance of scientific subject matter had often somehow been wholly lacking. Indeed the schoolbook order usually reverses things. It starts with generalizations, then tests the student's grasps with detailed problems and examples, and lets romance evaporate. So it was that our offerings were often aimed toward a rekindling of what in Whitehead's sense may be called the romance of subject matter, going on to some probing and exploration of detail, from which finally generalization might begin to take shape.

I should emphasize that these courses were not courses in pedagogy, in "teacher training." The topics we offered and materials we provided were for teachers' own learning. They were generally of a kind, however, that could be translated into classroom settings. One of the first courses that continued to attract teachers, nonthreateningly, was that of weaving, braiding, vegetable dying—the weaver's trade as humankind has long known it. Coming perhaps with an initial interest in making a belt or a purse, teachers soon found themselves faced with romance—the need to explore and experiment with the materials of one of our oldest technologies. This involved such matters as the uses and properties of animal and vegetable fibers, the mathematics of warp and weft or of the single-element braiding patterns, American Indian life, and much more. There were field trips to gather natural dyes, experiments with mordants and indicators to test fastness and color change. Teachers learned to make their own simple looms of many kinds and experiment with color patterns. There were offshoots like paper making and paper marbling. Living near our Southwestern Native American world we pursued opportunities to learn something about the sophistication of the "new" world's more ancient life and technology, still alive in many of our Indian communities. To "study Indians" is a traditional topic in American schools, often brief and stereotyped. There is also a tradition of craft work left over from the times of earlier educational reforms, but usually perceived as peripheral to more central matters called "academic." Our work was intended to suggest the ways in which these and other crafts could be far more central, more *academic* indeed, radiating their influence throughout the curriculum.

Other courses were enjoyed early and were of continuing popularity, such as horticultural studies of "plants in the classroom." Through the professional knowledge of one staff member we evolved a simple herbarium that gave teachers the materials for many kinds of classroom work with plants: studying pattern and propagations, nurture and growth, and with a wide variety of interesting species. Here again there was opportunity for teachers to realize that a neglected plant in a schoolroom window could evolve into a far more decorative and educational topic.

We also offered opportunities for the care and study of small animals in the classroom. We maintained two indoor ponds. One contained a muddy bank for salamanders. A visitor had brought us these, and we kept them for years as our mascots. Helping to feed them their diet of mealworms, one normally troubled but now fascinated young preschool visitor, looking at the mealworm he held, exclaimed suddenly, "Hey, you're an aminal (sic) too!" Respectful care and study of small animals can be for children a profound introduction to an understanding of humanity's place. On another occasion, when our salamanders were visitors in a Headstart preschool,

> Three salamanders with their expert tunneling and friendly ways transformed their terrarium for us all. "If you were a salamander," said a child one morning to a visitor, "would you want someone to pull you outta your hole? . . . No? . . . Well, then . . . you see" (he beamed slowly as he encompassed the terrarium with outstretched arms), "this is a salamander country!" In our salamander country you put your clean wet hand flat in the earth and if a salamander crawls into it you pick it up. (Hawkins & Kellogg, 1973, p. 24)

Another pond was for the profuse life, macroscopic and microscopic, borrowed and maintained with trips to a small nearby lake. And with advice from an expert field biologist we learned to maintain and study a "mouse country," just as we had for salamanders. Ample in scale with good soil for burrows, the cage grew grass to be cropped from uneaten seed, and was odor-free. In the same preschool young children learned some mouse diet and behavior, and the obligations and pleasures of maintenance. There evolved also a larger country for two guinea pigs, so rich in guinea pig attractions that although it was unfenced, they never left it. There was a course on animals in the classroom, with subjects ranging from guinea pigs to hydras and water fleas maintained in large petri dishes.

But much of this was, we feared, too great a challenge for many busy teachers. Fearing neglect by them, and so a loss of involvement by their children, we undertook the writing of a pamphlet, *"Don't* Have Animals in your Classroom unless. . . ."* Frances Hawkins formulated a parallel: A good classroom world for animals is only possible in a classroom which is a good world for children.

Help for Teachers in Math and Science

In all of these courses there are opportunities for math and science, as there were, for example, in our work in sound and music. But we also offered courses with the explicit labels of science and math. At first most of our teachers rather conspicuously avoided them. After a time they realized that these courses differed in style and in content from their stereotypes: kites and balloons, batteries and bulbs, heat and temperature, plant growth and reproduction, animal behavior, all involved much experimentation with simple materials, with much discussion and little lecturing. It was our hope that our teachers could become involved in such subjects and excited about them; with mainly their native common sense for background, this would lead them toward ways of teaching that for most at first would be be quite new and strange. Having enjoyed their own learning in this style they might have the background knowledge, and above all the courage, to help translate that background into classroom practice. So we hoped. These courses were indeed geared to what is or could well be elementary school subject matters, but they were not courses in pedagogy—except, we hoped, by example and informal talk. Working as we did in small groups intensively, there was of course much professional talk along the way. If we heard remarks like "My children could do this!", we might offer further help outside the course.

Math and physical science were avoided for contrasting reasons. Whereas science has been mostly absent from our schools, teachers are sternly committed to "mathematics"; to the routine practices, that is, of symbol manipulation and computation. This is what the ancient Greeks called "logistic," to contrast it with "arithmetic," which was the *science* of number, from which logistic could be derived. For most teachers, as for their children, this logistic is an interminable engagement with schoolbooks, routine excercises preparing for routine tests. For a few it holds no terrors. They are amateurs who love mathematics and whose children, most of them, can keep up with the required syllabus in a third of the time allotted, and spend the balance of it in genuinely mathematical constructions and investigations (see pp. 125–128). Teachers first avoided our math offerings, I conjectured, because they rightly thought that work with us should be enjoyable, and could not imagine that math could be so. The science courses were avoided mainly, I believe, because of a phobia acquired in their own schooling and because their teaching of it, if any, was from school-books with pictures of demonstrations and vocabulary exercises disguised as explanations.

In both sorts of courses we invited teachers into an investigative way of observing and questioning, postponing formal argument and learned explanation by trying to respect and amplify teachers' own questions and explanatory offerings. So it was that after a time the word got around; we then had sometimes to limit the numbers admitted. Disciplining ourselves to avoid the standard didacticism of math and science teaching, we tried to establish a pattern of work in which these subjects could be enjoyable and exciting.

It was from this background, combined with earlier teaching experience and with borrowings from colleagues elsewhere, that we evolved our curricular offerings, passing them on to teachers, encouraging them to select, to modify, and to add from their own developing interests and experience. In the following pages I have given a summary of three of these collections, together with some indications and case histories of their use. The selection of these particular topics is not intended to represent the wide range of matters potentially accessible to the elementary school. Rather, it reflects the limitations of my own experience, the contexts from which I have myself learned the most about early learning, and about the refreshment of topics often treated, rather disdainfully, as needing no further investigation. There are many others that stand in need of this sort of careful resuscitation, especially from biology. In a small pamphlet from our Center, Abraham Flexer (now its director) described the classroom preparation for a semester-long or year-long investigation of an elegant sample of the decay cycle, the vital and much neglected half of our planet's loop of recycling its resources. It is a mason jar suitably covered and half filled with horse manure, kept on a shelf in the classroom for careful daily observation and multiple spin-offs for added investigations and readings. Let me mention also a rich source, so far largely untouched for many biological phenomena accessible at elementary school levels and much prized, also, among present-day investigators. This book is about the growth and form of organisms, a classic of the 20th century (Thompson, 1942).

I mention D'Arcy Thompson's classic, also, because it gives a special emphasis to a badly needed and I believe quite central reconstruction in both mathematics and science education, and which my own final examples are intended to suggest. Thompson's work is a classic because he saw and brought together, or himself found, many important uses of mathematics—usually quite elementary mathematics from different branches—in visualizing and understanding the relations of morphology and embryology, of "growth and form." Logarithmic spirals in the growth of snail shells and Fibonacci numbers in leaf and stem arrangement are two more or less familiar examples, and there are many other. Esthetically captivating, these are entryways into the union of mathematics and biological form. I cannot make the full argument here, but it is part of the salvation of mathematics in the elementary curriculum that we abandon its disseverment from the wealth of nature's habits (Hawkins, 1973) and the early separation, within mathematics itself, of its arithmetical anf geometrical aspects. Sometime later in the curriculum, and all along the way, for some occasions and some children, specialization is needed and can be attractive. But mathematics has its essential roots in the world of nature and not in the computational algorithms which dominate so much of schooltime math. And where the roots are, that is where the learning should begin!

The examples that follow are chosen from parts of the spectrum in which I have some experience, with children and with their teachers. Of course they also reflect the limitations of my own background; others choose differently, even with the same intent. My examples are also chosen to reflect my own commitment to the "nondisseverment" of science and math. They may deviate somewhat from standard expectations about a book in *science* education. I might use them equally well as propaganda for those concerned with math teaching. But that is a larger order.

In the three topics I have chosen I have tried to suggest in some detail the ways in which good clusters of classroom materials can support investigations that a teacher wishes to provoke and guide. The uses teachers can make of them will vary with age and much else. I would hope, however, that teachers themselves could master them at adult levels of understanding, and enrich this understanding by an appreciation of children's own responses.

CONTENT AND STYLE: THREE EXAMPLES

The first example is of a subject matter in which arithmetic and geometry—and much else—can meet, one so "elementary" that the history of schooling has mainly passed it by. It is very close to the "pebble mathematics" of the early Greeks, investigated a century or more before Euclid's textbook "reduced it to order." The second example is the subject matter of balance, which belongs first to physics but then also to geometry and arithmetic, as all physics seems to do. The third topic is that of light and vision and color, relating equally to geometry and physics, and to the study of perception.

The Geometry and Arithmetic of Pebbles

I start with a collection of materials for classroom use. It is part of a larger collection, one evolved around the primary purpose of equipping children for mathematical investigations of many kinds. I limit myself to this partial collection because it relates to a cluster of investigations of which I have some experience, working with children of various ages and also with their teachers. It is a cluster I particularly value because it relates both to arithmetic and geometry, each of which can be a powerful aid in understanding the other. Here is the list:

smooth stream pebbles, many;
marbles, many;
plastic discs ("poker chips"), many of several colors;
geoboards and rubber bands;
a large pegboard (hardboard with square grid of holes) and many pegs
    (e.g., golf tees);
graph paper, large sheets;
polygonal tiles cut from vinyl flooring, many (see later);
the same, but of stiff card (see later);
folding metal mirrors (two hinged with tape);
equilateral triangles (about 30 cm. on an edge) of rigid transparent
    plastic; and
Cuisenaire rods and other standard concrete math materials.

In speaking of the relation between arithmetic and geometry, and of young children's access to them, one might begin, instead, with two other words, the hand and the eye. The eye is for the grasp of form, of shape and pattern. The hand is for doing and shaping, thus for form as well, but also for counts and measures. The digits of our arithmetical notation are the latin *digiti*, fingers of the two hands, two sets of five, as in either the Chinese abacus or the Roman numerals. Corresponding to the hand and the eye we have two ways of thinking, each powerful where the other is weak, the one holistic, the other step-by-step.

In searching some years ago for the causes and cures of the math phobia so prevalent among adults (including teachers), I noticed a few curious bits of evidence about the education of the latter. Under the guise of showing them some interesting work with children, I would involve them in that same work. I found that among quite a few there seemed to be a total lack of connection in their minds between some simple ideas of arithmetic and of geometry. The first example came with the word "square". Applied to shapes it was clearly understood, though not always sharply distinguished from "rectangle". In arithmetic it was known as a verb but not as an adjective. My friends knew, that is, that 5 × 5 is "five squared," but they could not recognize the "squareness" of the numbers in the sequence 1, 4, 9, 16, 25. . . . The one word thus had two meanings, seemingly unrelated. Needless to say, none of those friends were carpenters! But all did recognize the connection, as if with surprise, when it was shown them. I believe my own surprise, at their surprise, was greater; but anyone who explores carefully will also discover some far-reaching implications of this separation between our two most basic modes of representation. In a course on ecology for undergraduates, which required some practice in estimation, most of our undergraduate students had major difficulties in making use of areas and volumes as geometrical realities and, at the same time, numerical measures. They knew the dimensions of a football field but could not find the measure of its area. The relevant ideas were stored somewhere in their minds, for this or that practical use, but had never come together.

I can give other examples, and develop some later. But first I put forward a rather bold and simple thesis: Mathematics itself, in any of its many branches, is the joint offspring of hand and eye, of the union of our two basic modes of thought, when—and only when—these are joined together. Mathematical formalism may later develop that conceals this connection, but history reveals it. So I believe does a study of children's learning. On the other hand it is just this connection that has been lost in the tradition of the schools. In the elementary schools the dominant subject matter is computational arithmetic, in which the pictorial powers of the mind are reduced down to the reading and writing of the meager symbolic code. In high schools, geometry may have its day, but the course deals mainly with those parts of Euclid least obviously connected with numbers.

Thus, if the chemical reaction between number and form that gives rise to mathematical thinking ever occurs, it does so only incidentally along the way, and too late for many of us. There is historically a reason for this separation, but it is the expression of a concern for formal logical development that invalidly erases some of the pathways along which basic ideas have developed in the past, or along which a novice can enter the subject today.

This concern, which in my view has had such bad consequences, is an expression of the fact that the arithmetic of the natural numbers can find many geometrical representations limited to what I have called pebble geometry, shapes and patterns made of pebbles, coins, plastic discs, marbles, bricks, and so on—identical small objects grouped together to make interesting configurations. The Pythagoreans, a century or more before Euclid, had understood that all the arithmetic of the natural numbers—what we try to teach in the first few years of school—can be understood in terms of the two basic operations, of addition and multiplication. In their investigation they noticed, moreover, that all numbers, though generated merely by successive addition, could be grouped in geometical patterns. Thus with 3, 6, 10, . . . coins or poker chips one may form triangular patterns, or with 4, 9, 16, . . . the squares. The product of two numbers greater than 1 is similarly a rectangle. Some numbers will form many different rectangles, such as 24 = 2 × 12 = 3 × 8 = 4 × 6, while others form no rectangles—hence named the "primes." They found what we would call algebraic formulas for numbers of each class, connecting formula and shape. Numbers with three or more divisors also correspond, in this pebble geometry, to box shapes; where they can be factored into three indentical divisors, the box is a cube. Playing with these pebble-patterns and noticing their properties, the Greeks discovered some remarkable facts of arithmetic, or of geometry, or of both (Thomas, 1951). Thus, for example, the famous Pythagorean theorem of geometry is also a fact about an infinite class of number triples.

The logical difficulty with all of this, discovered by the Greeks, was that while the arithmetic of the natural numbers can be translated into geometry, the reverse translation requires a more generalized number system. They learned that there is no unit of measure (no "pebble," however tiny) in terms of which one can exactly measure both the side and the diagonal of a square. The Greeks actually met this difficulty but in doing so brought about the separation I object to in early education.

My main examples of ways to restore the linkage of hand and eye are from the later years of elementary school, or from work with teachers. There are, however, a few remarks that apply at all levels. One of these is the need for concrete representation of the numbers and their patterns in advance of being put to the task of learning our shorthand and quite arbitrary notation for these numbers and our operations with them. The uses of pebbles and other such tokens automatically relate the number to visual forms and manual operations and make it impossible, for example, to confuse addition and subtraction, or multiplication and division, two kinds of errors that are absurdly common when note-memorized notational rules have replaced elementary understanding.

My first example concerns the triangular numbers and the squares. Given a basket of plastic discs (poker chips) one invites the construction of patterns on a table top. This may lead to many kinds of patterns, some of which are representational, some purely geometrical. One of the latter is a sequence of "triangles." A first challenge is to write the number of chips in each as it is built—1, 3, 6, 10. . . . A second challenge is to guess the number in the next larger triangle, before it is built. At some point, moreover, one may see the general number pattern, and can announce what the number will be for some even much larger triangle. There are several nice ways of "seeing" this result, all genuine discoveries. And there are others. Thus, two successive triangles can be rearranged to form a square. Potential discoveries are endless, some recapitulating those of the early Greeks, others of which will relate to much later developments.

A further step of the same kind involves three-dimensional number patterns, for which I have used the large plastic triangles previously listed. Three of these can be taped together to form a three-sided pyramid, the regular tetrahedron, with one side open. Four of them similarly form half of the regular octahedron, and five form a corner of the regular 20-sided shape, the icosahedron. Each of these pyramids, point-down in a cardboard cylinder, makes a container in which we can stack marbles of uniform size. Filling them carefully, layer by layer, one generates quite elegant crystal shapes. (Note, in this account, the similarities with Schwartz's story cited by Duckworth, chapter 2, p. 21.) Keeping count of the numbers in successive layers can again lead to challenges, related to those generated by the poker-chip patterns, but somewhat more difficult. These numbers, in turn, lead also to some purely geometrical insight and understanding. Many of Euclid's theorems on areas and volumes for example, state facts which were first discovered, I believe, by such experimental means. In the world of later mathematics these same number patterns reappear, quite mysteriously, in other contexts, such as the famous triangle of numbers we name after Tartaglia or Pascal, but that was also known to the ancient Chinese. In that connection they are important in many other applications. Students who have met these numbers in one elementary connection can meet them again later and greet them as old friends— puzzling, perhaps, over their universality, and so raising deeper questions.

Quite different geometrical patterns emerge from the uses of tiles cut from vinyl floor material by means of the school's cutting board. Adults can easily manufacture large numbers of these, making use of master triangular guides that allow the blade to cut the vinyl at predetermined angles. Thus, a 30–60° draftsman's triangle will allow the cutting of equilateral triangles and hexagons. With other such guides one can produce other shapes. Squares, of course, need no extra guide. Regular pentagons require a guide with an 18° angle. Shapes can be cut with a common edge length. Having large numbers of these to play with, and with some often necessary adult investment, children can find many interesting patterns to support their ongoing curiosity. They soon learn that the triangles, squares, or hexagons can tile—can cover completely—the area they are laid on. One may also discover—usually with some surprise—that pentagons will not do so, but will go together, edge to edge, leaving holes of interesting shapes, including the familiar five-pointed star. Used together the squares and hexagons will also refuse to tile, leaving holes that can be filled with a third shape, a rhombus.

In the background of this work are the tesselated designs of the Alhambra in Spain (see p. 22). We ourselves have seen such patterns generated by children, using our materials, which are not put to shame. Because the vinyl floor material can be obtained in different colors one may produce, sometimes, a complex of interlacing patterns that are easy to see but too complex to analyze, aesthetically and mathematically appealing. There is an arithmetic and geometry that these patterns make available. The shapes constrain them. Thus, most adults and children do not at first seem clearly to distinguish the pentagon from the hexagon. Put together they force a recognition of their differences; each has a will of its own! And after much play of this kind there can be some "extending of our experience"—to quote Bohr once more—in directions which will suggest and underline important new ideas—of symmetry and order for example—perhaps to be explicitly developed later. Kaleidoscopic symmetries enter here also, made by the folding mirrors.

These same shapes offer another avenue of engagement. Cut from cardboard just thick enough to be rigid, they can be glued together to form various polyhedral solids. Two edges are easily joined by a thin bead of ordinary white glue, after being held together for a short time, then set aside for a somewhat longer time to cure. The art is challenging and not too hard to learn, while the solids that can be produced and colored are impressive. There are several good books on the subject, for amateurs.

Added to such constructions there is an architectural activity, one suggested to me by the late George Polya: simple perspective drawings of fairly regular three-dimensional shapes, starting with the cube (which all can draw), on graph paper or with a square guide. What can you draw inside this cube—a house, a tent? For geometry you have the cube already. Now, using a straightedge, mark the midpoint of each of the six square faces. Draw straight lines connecting each midpoint to its four neighbors. You have made a drawing of the octahedron inside the cube! You can erase the edges of the cube, for visibility, or just darken those of the octahedron. It is the shape of the elegant purplish fluorite crystals you have seen in rock shops. And now a challenge: Can you draw a (smaller) cube inside the octahedron? Starting again with the cube, what other interesting shapes can you draw?

Associated with all this geometry of solid shapes is a famous discovery called Euler's Theorem, which connects the numbers of edges, vertices and faces of any convex polyhedron. This curious bit of geometrical arithmetic, once found or pointed out, is a challenge again, to invent new polyhedral shapes to test it by. I recall a 12-year-old who "removed" a corner from the cube she had drawn and then found, with excitement, that for both of the solid shapes thus produced the number of edges was two less than the number of faces plus corners, as Euler's rule requires. "I am convinced," she announced. Did she have "an idea for a proof"?

There are many other uses of the materials in the collection I have listed, and many other sorts of materials that can be brought together for the mathematics laboratory of a classroom or school. The subject is rich enough to support a wide diversity of choice, both of teachers' repertoires and children's interests. I hope that I have amply illustrated the wealth of cross-connections between the eye and the hand, form and number, out of which mathematics arose historically and can be regenerated in the minds of children and their teachers. The conceptual barriers to the learning of mathematics often lie (if I am correct) in our traditional failure to exploit these cross-linkages, which can both extend our experience and help find ways of ordering it.

I hope also that I have suggested the kinds of knowledge and acquaintance with mathematical subject matter that teachers can genuinely profit by, either from their previous education or as work in progress. I am afraid it is usually lacking from the former source, and too little supported in the latter. A spirit of playfulness wins half the battle, and that above all needs our support. The other half, which I believe must accompany it, is help in suggesting ways in which children's potential mathematical interests can be noticed, supported, and extended. With such support the teachers' own understanding and repertoire can continue to grow, to grow away both from phobia and from boredom. There is no single royal road to competence and understanding in elementary mathematics. But there can be good road maps that give schools and teacher, and then children, significant choices for learning. I hope, finally, that my examples make it clear why there should be no separations in the early years, between mathematics and the rest of what we call science (Hawkins, 1973). See also the story about "Carla" that opens Duckworth's chapter.

The Physics and Mathematics of Balance

There are many simple materials for the study of balance. Some require description, however, and I do not list them initially. Among practical arts the use of the balance (or the lever) is as primitive as weight lifting or as commerce. It is described in ancient literatures, but its first theoretical treatment appears to be that of Archimedes. It is often treated perfunctorily, and sometimes incorrectly, in the schoolbook tradition. Although it appears as a simple and rather restricted topic, it can reveal many riches for those who wish to explore it. As subject matter it belongs essentially to the beginnings of physics, and like many simple topics it can be deep.

I start with the design of mobiles. These became a form of decorative art in fairly recent times; the mobiles designed by Calder and others are elegant museum artifacts. Fine classroom mobiles are within the competence of children to build. They can embody different sorts of symmetry and equilibrium, obvious or hidden. They can be complex, but manageably so. A naturalistic example is a tree branch found after a windstorm, hung at the right point by a string from the ceiling or sitting on the sharp point of a standing support.

To manage the complexity of mobile construction there is but one essential strategy. Buildings are designed from the top down. For mobiles there is a similar same architectural principal. Children (and adults) can need some time to discover this, and need not to be robbed of the chance.

Armed with prior theory one may object to such beginnings, they express the phenomena of balance in a most complicated form. Should one not, instead, begin with the simplest case, as Archimedes does: two identical weights at equal distances from a point of support? In general such a configuration will *not* balance, but will fall by chance one way or the other. Adults and children may invest much care in trying to balance a board or ruler on a knife-edge support, as the schoolbook picture sometimes implies. But apart from this basic question of stability in equilibrium, there is another. I go back to the quotation from Niels Bohr. When experience has been extended, and ways found to reduce it to order, it is appropriate that this new ordering be developed in logical form, proceeding from simple to complex. The classical example, of course, is Euclid. That so much of geometry, of isolated facts independently discovered, could later be derived from a few simple generalities, was and remains a remarkable achievement. But the deductive ordering of its argument requires a readiness of understanding, of prior geometrical experience, which is often lacking. So with the phenomena of balance. Through massive daily experience, of a good many kinds, we all know something about balance, at a practical level. But to achieve a wider understanding we go generally in the backward direction, from complex to simple. Balance an artist's palette (or any odd shape made of hardboard) on a tennis ball in a cup, and play a game, taking turns to place weights on it, like steel washers, so that they don't slide off. Now reverse the game, with magnets to remove them. Build towers of kindergarten blocks that almost fall, but not quite. How far can you displace the top of such a tower from its base? Archimedes is always there, but there is no need for haste to make him explicit.

Children suitably challenged can invent many other forms of balance, and investigate the schoolyard see-saw with fresh interest, or boards on fulcrums, rounded or sharp-edged, in the classroom. Such a balance, with various sorts of weights distributed over it, is a challenge which can lay the groundwork for Archimedes' Law, and one far richer than the textbook formulation.

Archimedes investigations into the nature of balance, summarized in what today we call the "law of moments," were also used by him in several quite different ways. He used it, of course, for accurate weighing, as in the famous story of the king's crown. But he also used it for the discovery of new facts of geometry that had eluded his predecessors. Thus, he found the formulas for the surface area and the volume of a sphere, and did this by an argument that involved the imaginary slicing of the sphere into thin layers (as we slice an orange) and imagining the weighing of these against some corresponding sections of the cylinder and cone, for which the formulas were already known. The argument is difficult but there are simpler ones. We have thus made circles and diameters of soldering wire and balanced one against the other, sliding one back and forth on a simple sensitive meterstick balance, and found the ratio of their distances from the fulcrum about 3.14! Then we have weighed a cardboard circle against a square, one cut with an edge length equal to the radius of the circle. Lo and behold, when one is weighed against the other the ratio is again about 3.14. Those are the formulas most adults once learned from a book, then confused or forgot. The balance is also a nice way of finding irregular areas such as footprints, or of numerical integration—finding the area under a curve. Cut out the relevant area and compare its weight with that of a rectangle of the same graph paper!

I conclude this discussion of balance with one observation, one I only mentioned earlier. This is the great difficulty that learners can experience in understanding why some balance configurations, in which there is seemingly perfect equilibrium, will nevertheless prove impossible to maintain. We all do of course understand extreme cases, but they do not seem to help. We all know that you cannot balance a pencil on its point, no matter how carefully you try. And we can stand Columbus' egg on end only by cheating. We all understand the extreme opposite case, that of a ball sitting in the bottom of a rounded cup. These two kinds of simple situations can become powerful metaphors for understanding all kinds of more complex balance configurations, both stable and unstable. But to build this bridge of understanding we must first have built up a marvelous simplifying idea that of the *center of gravity*, or *center of mass*. This idea is that of a single point in space where, we can imagine, all the weight is concentrated—an ideal point that will be either above or below the actual fulcrum. Next we tilt our balance slightly. If the center of mass then rises, the situation is like that of the ball in the cup, and the equilibrium is stable. If the center of mass goes downward with tilting, the equilibrium is unstable, like the pencil on its point.

But to arrive at this idea is a creative act, and in our work—first with children, later with teachers—we have tried to lay the groundwork for such insights, ideas that can help us find simplicity in our understanding of nature. In this case we have sometimes invited our students to build "trees" out of tinkertoy spools and rods which will then balance on a finger. Very often the first efforts are failures, the trees persist in falling over until some special condition is met. I have a vivid memory of one valiant teacher to whom I had suggested this problem and who solved it after a persistent effort. She came to me finally and told me, with excitement, that it all depended on whether "that center point," a point "sort of halfway" between all those spools and rods, was *below* her finger, stable, or *above* it, unstable. Beaming, she then announced to me, "I have a *mind!*".

As teachers, we seldom know the long-run consequences, if any, of such creative steps our students take. But it is an obligation that when we chose materials and phenomena for them to investigate, we have, or seek to have, some sense of the riches of understanding which can grow if those investigations prove absorbing *and* are later recalled and extended. When we have gained these ideas, of the center of mass and of the stability of balance, we will have built up a model which is the first of an important series of similar ideas which have grown up in the sciences, ideas which have to do with questions of order and stability. If I am allowed some fanciful language I will say that topics like this one are on sacred ground.

Light and Vision

In our work with this topic we have used a variety of simple materials. Mirrors are essential; small ones of stainless steel or plastic are safer for children than glass. The best source of light, always and forever, is the sun (never of course to be looked at direct). For indoor work the sunlight may enter through a window or be piped in with an outdoor mirror. Lacking sunlight or in addition to it, school projectors will do. For colors there are plastic filters, the kind used in theatrical work, plastic or glass prisms, and gratings. Vivid rainbows can be manufactured in morning or afternoons with a fine spray from the garden hose, especially when seen against a dark shadowy background. Cheap lenses are in order for magnifiers, and two of them can make a telescope. But first, at least in my own order of things to study deeply, are shadows—whether for young children or adults (Elementary Science Study, 1966).

Shadows are universal, but close observation of them is not. Beyond the activities described in chapter 2 there are many more: Can you jump on to your own shadow? When are they long, when shortest? When you walk by a pond of still water, across from the evening or morning sun, you may find you have two shadows! Most children and even many adults are unclear about the geometrical relation between the light, the object, and its shadow; or that the shadow exists, unseen, between the object and the surface we see it on. How many shadow shapes can you make with a circle or square of cardboard; a cube? The sun-shadow of a tall pole is sharp near its base, and fuzzy at greater distances; a mystery for many. The phenomena are endless, although they almost all hover about a final, simple abstraction; that of the light ray may reduce them to order. But again we need the phenomena, closely observed and questioned, before the abstraction can come alive.

Mirrors are another endless source, as we began to see in chapter 2. Again we grow up taking them for granted, mostly. Kittens first think there is a kitten behind the mirror, and if Piaget had tried it his infants might have reacted similarly. A mirror is a special kind of hole or window, but our pragmatic interests, like a kitten's, soon lead us away from this basic notion. It gets treated as a kind of moving picture. Yet, mirror land is real; you cannot enter it, but only because you are already there. The mirror is a special kind of reversing window. Much investigation has shown that in our imagination we foreshorten that third dimension and see the mirror world as a 2-D picture (Apelman et al., 1981). Why else would it seem so surprising, as it does to many, that a mirror smaller than our head would show the whole head? Or that a camera we focus on ourselves will show a focal distance twice that of the camera from the mirror?

This topic of mirror vision comes close to the conceptual mystery I discussed earlier and that it may be wise, for a time, to avoid, the relation of light and vision. Small mirrors, used to reflect a beam of light around the room, are a safer topic. As with shadows the subject matter is geometrical optics, unaffected with questions about our seeing. If we use sunlight they can still lead away to another topic: astronomy. Place a small mirror at some distance outside a window, to put a spot of sunlight on an inside wall. I did this once to ask why the spot was round, rather than shaped like the rectangle of the mirror. What happened, however, was that the spot was suddenly seen to be *moving!* The diurnal motion of shadows, similarly, can be the beginning of a fine investigation of "daytime astronomy."

A large carton, of the sort in which refrigerators are shipped, will admit one or two children. Closed carefully against stray light, it makes a splendid camera obscura. A hole at one end can be covered with foil in which we can try small holes of various sizes. Pointed toward some interesting scene it will produce images inside on white paper. Such a large image is faint, and requires minutes of dark adaption to see it, even then without color. A small lens of suitable long focal length gives much brighter images, in color. As a 5-year-old child, hiding from sisters, I saw such an image, by chance, from a hole in the outside wall of a dark closet in a primitive mountain cabin, and the memory is still strong. Such phenomena are on the edge of everyday experience, and they can extend it. *Why* is the "picture" upside down? If one adds a little action to this picture, even the people are upside down! It is at this point that one usually makes a very simple drawing, straight lines from the top and bottom of a sketch of a house or tree, through the pinhole and on to the screen. More often than not this explanation is received with no clear sign of enlightenment. For many it presupposes just what it purports to explain: the concept of a "picture" which is only there by rectilinear projection of what we then call "light rays." Especially in the modern world, one might think, the experience of pictures maintained by projection is so common that everyone must of course understand it. On the contrary we find much evidence that this understanding is partial at best. For many this simple "explanation" involves a major conceptual restructuring. We are on to a splendid example of the way in which common *sense* can accept and categorize common *experience* without curiosity or close observation. Although geometrical optics provides a conceptual frame that unifies the description of a host of everyday optical phenomena (and to new mysteries as well) it seems clear that verbal and diagramatic explanations do not by themselves suffice. The common difficulties about shadows and mirrors—and cameras—can easily be resolved by geometrical optics, but often do *not* do so without a special kind of struggle. It is not that the conception of rectilinear propagation is wholly lacking; it is itself accessible in some cases, for example in describing the single or multiple reflection of a beam of sunlight with small mirrors, or in other such applications. Is the light "transmitted," much like a stream of particles? Why is the analogy of propagation accessible here, but not in other cases? There is still one more phenomenon to mention that sharpens this question and suggests an answer.

With a group of teachers we played with the phenomena of additive color mixing. With three simple projectors and colored filters we spent quite a bit of time with these phenomena. They proved to be very exciting, because they were unfamiliar and quite unlike the mixing of pigments. With two or three overlapping pools of light we produced many colors, white included. A hand held in the lights produced extraordinary shadow patterns, and finally produced a nice puzzle: why, with two lights, is the shadow from the red light green, and from the green light red? Here again there was unexpected difficulty. Although the role of the projectors was "obvious," the color patterns on the wall were apparently seen as colors *on*, or *of*, the wall and *not* in their projective character. Hence the puzzlement; or so I believe.

I do not discuss the array of evidence for my interpretation of all these learning phenomena, but I believe others can and should reproduce them in working with children or with scientifically naive adults, and try to interpret them independently. My own interpretation suggests a remarkable parallel with the history of geometrical optics, which I previously referred to. For this one should see the classic history of Vasco Ronchi (1957), *Optics, The Science of Vision* and Gerald Holton (1973) *Thematic Origins of Scientific Thought*.

Throughout that long history it is abundantly clear that there is an apparent contradiction between the way in which we describe the transmission of light and the way in which we describe vision. I spoke of this previously (pp. 106–108). When we think of our visual perception of physical objects the objects themselves, out in front of our eyes, are what normally we *directly* perceive. In this sense the act of vision is one which reaches out to the object much as the hand and fingers do in tactile perception. The subject of *light* enters then only as a condition of vision; light as opposed to darkness. Indeed in some ancient discussions darkness is thought of nicely as a space-filling opacity that prevents "the ray of the eye" from reaching out to its object. The role of the sun or the lamp is then to dispel this opacity, to push it out of the way and thus allow the eye to reach the object. On the other hand the sun or the lamp produce and *transmit* light, it is *sent out* rectilinearly from the source. But now suppose that someone directs the beam of a bright flashlight into our eyes. Will our "native common sense" say that the eye reaches out to the flashlight, or on the contrary that the light is transmitted into our eyes? Many years ago, a class of fourth-grade children decided that in seeing an apple, the ray of the eye reached out to the apple; but that in the case of the flashlight, the light came *to* the eye. In both cases they had accepted the idea of the straight-line ray: The eye could not see around a corner, nor could light be so transmitted. To establish this they had used a length of rigid plastic tubing, looking through it at various objects and shining lights through it into the eyes. But then they were confronted with tubing which had a bend in the middle. The eye could not get through, the light could not get through! In describing the experience they said (with considerable agreement) that the two rays *met* there. A splendid compromise! It is, once more, a compromise you can find in history; those children were reinventing a scheme proposed in ancient times, by Plato. My report of it came from a colleague, M. L. Sherburne.

In this case history of light and vision one can see that a major restructuring of thought has to evolve in order that geometrical optics can be well learned and understood. That this should be so, of such an "elementary" subject matter, may seem surprising at first—to those who already understand it! But when we bring forth the common sense accomodations to the rich array of visual phenomena, and the possible ways in which a simple geometry can unify them, we should no longer be surprised.

CONCLUSION

In this chapter I was concerned with certain problems of education in science and mathematics, for children of ages 5–12, and with closely related problems in the early and continuing education of teachers. I began by stating two principal sources of difficulty to be overcome in science and mathematics teaching generally, and especially in the help we offer to teachers of the young. These are difficulties in bridging the gaps between the common sense understanding of the world and that which is scientifically informed, even—I would say especially—at what are considered to be quite elementary scientific levels.

To describe these difficulties I relied on a brief observation by the great physicist Niels Bohr. The aim of science, he said, is to *extend* our experience and *reduce* it to order. As we extend our experience, Bohr said, it is necessary, along the way, to invent new points of view from which that reduction to order can be achieved. In the Chapter I gave examples of this conceptual restructuring and of the difficulties in achieving it. In recent years it has been a subject of much research. This research has shown that conventional science teaching has not succeeded in helping learners, young or old, to overcome such "conceptual barriers." It also points strongly toward ways of teaching which bring students into an active, investigative atmosphere and frame of mind.

A second observation from Bohr is his Principal of Correspondence, which states that when such new points of view are found, they must be themselves developed and tested by the measure of their continuity with older points of view, those which have proved to be adequate in describing phenomena from a more limited range of experience. For educational purposes I renamed this as the Principle of the Conservation of Common Sense. By *common sense* I mean any way of describing and thinking about natural phenomena which has become habitual for the learner. It is entirely possible that students can learn new ways of describing natural phenomena presented to them in science courses, and yet never learn to relate these to their previous experience. Such learning is then often superficial and transitory, it lacks that *connectedness* that allows it to become a permanent resource of the mind.

In a second part of the chapter I gave a rather personal account of experience in teaching "almost adult" university students. I did this mainly as a way of suggesting how Bohr's Correspondence Principle can become a rather powerful pedagogical tool.

In a third part of the chapter I summarized some of our work with children and with elementary school teachers who have enlisted in our courses. In these courses we have introduced topics and materials that have also been well used in work with children. The first was one to which I gave the title "Pythagorean mathematics," the geometry and arithmetic of pebbles used as counter and as units of structure. The second was the topic of balance, which has many aspects and many degrees of richness. The third was that of light and vision, which most clearly illustrates what we believe we have learned.

I have alluded to an early observation of Paolo Guidoni, that those who have been badly taught in science will, in general, teach it badly. Because most of us in modern societies have been taught science badly, the implications of this remark are pessimistic. I regard it as valid, but only in a first approximation. Throughout the chapter I tried to develop a kind of second approximation. In this second approximation we must recognize that even those who have been taught a great deal of science may nevertheless teach badly for the early years, and that some who know relatively little may teach it well. My numerous examples are intended to suggest how this can be true. At the most elementary (and important) levels of scientific understanding, teachers can learn to teach well, not because they know a great deal of the science that is in the textbooks, but because they have learned some of the art of supporting children's own curiosities and investigations, and because they know how to share in and learn from those investigations.

To teach in this way does not initially require great scientific background, although that is always valuable. It is, however, an art that quite essentially needs much professional recognition and help. My final plea, more fully developed elsewhere, is that we find ways of offering far more of that kind of support than is at present available (Hawkins, 1983).

In this book we all are writing about the learning and teaching of science, about "science education" for children and for their teachers. So we have distinguished science from other phases of the curriculum. We do this because we believe that education for science—for a wider understanding of the order of nature—is profoundly needed in our world of today. We also all believe that there are special problems, *and special opportunities*, connected with any deeper penetration, into our schools, of the spirit and substance of the sciences.

But what about the rest of the curriculum? By and large we have been silent about it, writing as we should from our somewhat specialized personal experience. Yet this silence could be taken to mean that what we have to say about science teaching has no pertinence to the rest of early schooling—thus to the learning and teaching of writing and reading, of the social studies and history, of the choice-making talents of children, their ethical understanding. I think I speak for all of us in saying that this interpretation of our silence would be quite wrong. If there are special problems and opportunities in the enlargement of science teaching, success there can hardly fail to add new impetus toward more general improvements in early schooling. Thus, we join forces with all who seek to enliven our classrooms and extend their powers. Indeed to invest classrooms with some of the laboratory materials of early science and math is already a boost, along with those of children's expressive artistry, away from the sheer dominance ofprinted paper (*pace* the computer!) which our educational establishments have increasingly imposed.

A few years ago, after Frances Hawkins had spoken at an Oakland University course for teachers about young children's ways of learning, one teacher responded with a story. Returning to teaching after raising a family, she said, she had her husband and son bringing some of her favorite equipment to the new classroom, including a sand table and a water table. Seeing this, her principal spoke to her nervously: "You know, Mrs. _____ , our school has a strong *academic* emphasis." "Oh yes," she replied, "I couldn't teach *physics* without this equipment!" She later found piles of fill-in-the-blanks workbooks in her closet. Asking if she would be required to use them, she was told that indeed she must. "So," she said, "we used them. We weighed them singly and by twos and by threes. We weighed them dry and we weighed them wet."

Alas! In the United States the old kindergarten tradition, based on some understanding of children's development and their special talents for learning, has largely been replaced by a sweetly puritanical insistence on the "academics," defined somehow by those little workbooks and time-on-task exercises. The re-introduction of the investigative and playful spirit of science, into the equations of early schooling, could indeed help us create a better climate there for learning other things as well. In expressing this hope we must also, I am sure, remain wary of the dangers of increased pressure toward what might be called fill-in-the-blanks science! All of us have found reason to criticize the dominance, for later grades, of our purely textbookish kind of science. Textbooks used to be understood, and still should be, as books for reference, not as defining the curriculum; supporting teachers' initiatives, not replacing them.

For myself, then, I would add only one final comment. The extraordinary history of the sciences, the way they have changed the world, has created the gap we seek to bridge between their substance, their ways of thought, and the common understanding of those outside their domains. Part of this gap seems to me to have been unavoidable. But part not: along the way there has grown up a kind of mystique, affecting all of us, even scientists themselves, which conceals the roots of science within the common understanding, its continuity with what I have meant by the term "common sense." In a world better accommodated to what we now call science that word itself, that invidious label, might well have disappeared from use: a needless synonym for what was known, for ways of using that knowledge: for enjoyment, for increasing its substance, and for the planetary welfare.

REFERENCES

Apelman, M., Colton, R., Flexer, A., & Hawkins, D. (1981). *A Report of research on critical barriers to the learning and understanding of elementary science.* Boulder, CO: Mountain View Center, University Museum, University of Colorado.

Apelman, M., Hawkins, D., & Morrison, P. (1985) *Critical barriers phenomena in elementary science.* Grand Forks, ND: North Dakota Study Group on Evaluation,

Center for Teaching and Learning, University of North Dakota.

Bohr, N. (1934) *Atomic theory and the description of nature.* Cambridge: Cambridge University Press.

Driver, R., Guesne, E., & Tiberghien, A. (Eds.). (1985). *Children's ideas in science.* Milton Keynes, UK: The Open University Press.

Elementary Science Study. (1966). *Light and shadow.* New York: McGraw Hill.

Hawkins, D. (1973). *Nature, man and mathematics.* Paper presented at the second International Congress on Mathematics Education, Exeter, England.

Hawkins, D. (1983). Nature closely observed. In S. Graubard (Ed.), *Scientific literacy, Daedalus* (Vol. 12). Proceedings of the American Academy of Arts and Sciences.

Hawkins, F. (1975). Jack's world. In *Outlook* (Vol. 40, pp. 3–16). Boulder, CO: Mountain View Publishing.

Hawkins, F., & Kellogg, B. (1973). Work in progress: a room at Head Start. In *Outlook* (Vol. 9). Boulder, CO: Mountain View Publishing.

Hills, G. L. C. (1989). Students' "untutored" beliefs about natural phenomena: Primitive science or commonsense? Issues and trends. *Science Education 73* (2), 155–186.

Holton, G. (1973). *Thematic origins of scientific thought.* Cambridge, MA: Harvard University Press.

Minstrel, J. (1984). Teaching for the development of understanding of ideas: Forces on moving objects. In C. W. Anderson (Ed.), *Association for the education of teachers of science yearbook* (pp. 55–73).

Piaget, J. (1970). *Genetic epistemology* (E. Duckworth, Trans.). New York: Columbia University Press.

Ronchi, V. (1957). Optics, the science of vision (E. Rosen, Trans.). New York: New York University Press.

Thomas, I. (Ed.). (1951). *Greek mathematical works* (vol. 1). *From Thales to Euclid.* Cambridge, MA: The Loeb Classical Library.

Thompson, D. (1942). *Growth and form* (2 vols.). Cambridge and New York: Cambridge University Press.

Vicentini, M. (1980). Common sense knowledge and scientific knowledge. C. P. McFadden (Ed.), *World trends in science education* (pp. 276–281). Halifax, Nova Scotia: Atlantic Institute of Education.

Whitehead, A. N. (1949). *The aims of education.* New York: New American Library.

5

Experiments in Teaching

Androula Henriques
University of Geneva

The necessity of teaching natural sciences and particularly experimental sciences at primary and pre-primary school levels is generally acknowledged. However, the question still remains as to what the content of such teaching should be and which teaching method would be most suitable.

In deciding on the content, two factors come into play:

1. The body of knowledge that makes up what is currently accepted as official science. What one teaches should constitute a foundation for what is taught at secondary school and university.
2. The child's ability to learn. It is obvious that one cannot teach anything at any age and it is now becoming equally evident that one cannot teach anything anyhow.

In the choice of a method of teaching several factors have to be taken into account, among them:

- One of the most important is the role of the teacher that is traditionally the pivotal role in the classroom. The teacher is the reservoir of scientific knowledge that is transmitted to his or her pupils with his or her pedagogical skill. The teacher structures the lesson on a theme of his or her choice, guides the ignorant, punishes the deviant, and so forth. Attempts to change this role meet with obstacles that are difficult to overcome. Certain schools of psychology attribute great importance to the learner and advocate a different role for the teacher; one with less power, one that is more subtle and difficult to play. This change is clearly not welcomed either by the school or by parents.

- A second factor, complementary to the previous, is the theoretical frame of reference, the psychopedagogy upheld. The actors are not always conscious of this frame of reference, making dialogue between researchers, educationists, and teachers difficult. Due to the diversity of theoretical frameworks, the same teaching practice may appear valid to some and dangerous to others. Thus, some may consider the spontaneous representations of the child an obstacle to teaching, whereas others regard them as constructs that must be respected.

We hope that the study presented here contributes toward clarifying the two questions just raised:

- What "science" should be taught to children between the ages of 7 and 12?
- What method should be adopted for teaching this content?

The answers to these questions are of course interdependent: The content will in part determine the method and the method will in turn influence decisively the choice of content. Besides, the choice of both the content and the method depend, in our opinion, on the child, or rather, on one's conception of the child. It is of capital importance that those who work with children try to make explicit their ideas about children, both for their own benefit and for that of others. To describe one's conception in detail is a difficult task. Here, I present certain aspects of my own conception of the child that are relevant to science teaching.

My conception is inspired by Piaget. This does not mean that it is exactly the one that Piaget traced patiently and obstinately throughout his long life of research. It is Piagetian because I consider the child a being that constructs himself (i.e., not only his knowledge but also his intellectual tools) in continuous interaction with his surroundings. It fits in with the epistemological framework elaborated by Jean Piaget.

Through their own activities, children construct forms of organization that permit them to reduce the "chaos" that surrounds them and convert it into knowledge. This idea is typically Piagetian in that the actions of the subject are the source of knowledge. Piaget, however, in

creating the concept of "concrete operations" with the aim of empha-
sizing the importance of concrete objects as a support for operational
reasoning especially up to the age of 10, caused some of his followers
to erroneously identify "activity" with "manipulation." I therefore
wish to point out that when we talk of "activity" in the Piagetian
sense, we refer to mental activity that cannot be observed as such but
that can be inferred from observable indices furnished by the subject
(manipulation, verbal explanations, etc.).

An example of this follows. A person seeks to understand how two
mirrors reflect objects. The two mirrors are bound together with tape
that acts as a hinge permitting variations of the angle of aperture. The
observable manipulation is limited to a few movements: He places the
mirrors at different angles and places one or more objects in front of
them. The angle of aperture and the number of objects may be varied
more or less systematically. The underlying mental activity is not
directly observable.

Mental Activity

Limiting the child's activity to the manipulations performed would
mean that one considers the object as the main factor in the construction of knowledge. If the object were the main factor, we would be at a
loss to explain why the same objects manipulated yield such different
results in terms of the knowledge acquired. Coming back to the
experiment with the double mirror: Children ages 7 to 10 generally
deduce a qualitative law that they express somewhat like this: "The
more I close the mirrors, the more images I see." Some add that at first
they believed it to be the other way around. Many children perceive
that the objects are inverted, but very few can infer the rules of such
inversion. Adults (students of psychology) have no problems understanding the inverted image. They are also able to express a quantitative relationship between the number of images formed and the angle
of aperture between the mirrors.

This diversity observed in the same situation suggests that knowledge comes neither from the object directly nor from its manipulation.
It is the result of mental activity that varies from person to person
according to his or her level of development.

Let us now try to define what this activity consists of.

1. First, in a choice of a few or several *meaningful units* (i.e., a series
of subdivisions that the subject considers relevant to a given situation).
To put it more precisely, the learner attributes meaning by "*assimilat-*

ing" (in the Piagetian sense of the term) the subunits that he or she considers appropriate to the problem before him or her into previously constructed schemata. If, for example, one wishes to understand the inversion of the image in the mirror, the significant units chosen will be quite different from those one would choose in understanding the relationship between the number of images, the number of objects and the angle of aperture. Simultaneously with this subdivision, the learner establishes relationships between the units concerned, the manipulations performed, and the "responses" of the object. He or she classifies, seriates spatially and temporally, and co-ordinates these. In our example, the child seriates the angles between the mirrors according to their aperture and makes this series correspond to the variations of the number of images of the object placed in front of the double mirror.

Another aspect of mental activity is its inferential nature. On the basis of these relationships, the learner infers rules and regular occurences and constructs notions and concepts. To say, for example, that the number of images increases as the angle diminishes, is a proposition that expresses an inference and not just a description of a perceptual observation.

In the end, the mechnisms that check the adequacy of inferences, of relationships established, and the choice of significant units made, come into play. The learner may thus retrospectively modify these to a greater or lesser extent in various ways.

If we postulate, as earlier, that the choice of significant units of a situation is an essential aspect of mental activity, it follows that the "object" in the widest sense of the term (thing, verbal communication, simple or complex situation), can "enter into dialogue" with the learner only after being transformed by him or her. In fact, it is the set of significant units organized by the learner and the relationships that he or she constructs between them that constitutes the cognitive object that, in turn, constitutes knowledge.

2. Mental activity is more than just the construction of cognitive objects. As these are being constructed, the learner "explores," thinks about them, and "prolongs" their significance. The following examples illustrate this phenomenon:

> A set of nesting Russian dolls (seven hollow, wooden dolls that fit into each other) allows for a wide variety of activities. Small children are content with fitting them into each other. Toward the age of 6 or 7, children begin to seriate them according to their size thus creating a new toy, a new cognitive object to be explored.

"Exploring" seriation is different from doing it. It implies, among other things, being aware of the specific relationships involved, namely transitivity. This was brought out in an experiment conducted by the author in 1968 (A. Papert-Christofides, 1972).

One hundred children between the ages of 4 and 10 were tested individually. I showed them the upper half of six Russian dolls and asked them to seriate them. The youngest were helped to do this. Then the child was asked to close his eyes while the experimenter hid an object under doll No.3 (the biggest being No.1 and the smallest No.6). The experimenter then said: "I have hidden something here under this doll. Do you think I could have hidden it under this one (No.2)? And under this one (No.4)? What do you think? (The same questions were asked pointing to No.1, No.5 and No.6.) After the first few responses the child was asked if he was sure and why.

The responses obtained may be classified into three groups:

a. There are dolls under which one is sure that the object can be hidden—the "big ones." There are those under which one cannot hide the object—the "little ones." The dividing line between the two is usually between doll No.3 (the one under which the object is hidden) and doll No.4. But it can also be between No.4 and No.5 or between No.5 and No.6. The majority of children between 4 and 8 years old reply in this way and do not question their statements. The justification is simply: "because the doll is big" or "because the doll is small."

b. The second group of responses are those where the child begins to doubt: for certain dolls the child hesitates, cannot decide, is not sure if one could hide the object. The series is divided into three: big dolls under which one can certainly hide the object, small ones under which one cannot hide it, and the others for which one cannot be sure. Generally, dolls No. 4 and 5, and sometimes even No.2 are among the "others."

c. The third and most advanced group of responses were given by half of the 8-year-olds and by the large majority (20 out of 22) of 9- and 10-year-olds. They maintained that under dolls Nos. 1 and 2 one can hide the object "because they are bigger than doll No.3" and that one cannot say definitely for the dolls smaller than No.3 without more information about the size of the hidden object. What is peculiar is that a significant proportion of these children "seriate" their doubts and certitudes . . . thus some are more sure about Doll No.1 than about Doll No.2 and similarly for No. 6 as compared to No. 4.

This example shows that a given content (Russian dolls) can be organized in a certain way (seriation), but that being able to think about this form of organisation requires a certain period of time.

3. The significance of the cognitive object undergoes continuous modification. It is of pedagogical interest that the learner does not always "extend" objects in the manner that the teachers wish. Here are two examples of this:

Andre, age 4, learns from his father that the earth revolves around the sun. His father being a good teacher, the lesson was well delivered and apparently well received. The following day Andre asks his mother: "Has Dad been to the earth already?" The mother, a little surprised says "To the moon, you mean. No, he hasn't yet been to the moon." Andre insists, "No, to the earth, the real earth, the one that revolves around the sun. I know that the moon revolves around the earth, this earth on which we are." Andre had "prolonged" the cognitive object "earth" and made two of them. His father is not to blame for he could not have predicted such extension and if Andre had not happened to mention it, it would have gone unnoticed.

Fabio, a 24-year-old psychology student, volunteers for an experiment on heat and temperature. During the experiment, Fabio explains that, for him, temperature means movement—a statement that came as a pleasant surprise to us. The movement of the atoms and molecules of a body determines its temperature. When we asked how he pictured this movement, he said it was like water that was boiling. He then added that skis slide better on snow that is not very cold because "the molecules of snow being in motion help the movement of the skis like ball bearings." The college professor who introduced the kinetic interpretation of temperature to Fabio is, like Andre's father, not responsible for the extensions of the cognitive object "temperature" that Fabio extrapolated.

The Child's World

Children, in an effort to understand the world around them, organize, interpret, and explain it to themselves. Out of this process comes a body of ideas, beliefs, and theories that one could call child physics or biology. If we wish to enter this world constructed by children we must learn to listen to them and to talk to them without imposing or even suggesting our adult conceptions of the world. One is amazed and amused by their conceptions concerning the world: "The moon is following us," "The Saleve [a mountain] has come closer this morning because of the wind," and so on. Piaget (1926) cited several pictures-ques phrases of this kind collected from children below 5 years old.

Older children talk of other things in ways that are perhaps less unexpected. Here are some examples concerning the propagation of heat, light, and sound: Heat is transmitted by air. Hence, it cannot penetrate hard things like metal unless these have holes in them.

We gave primary school children in Geneva three rods, a glass rod, an iron rod, and a tin tube each about 20 cms long. Bits of wax were fixed at regular intervals along the rods. The children were asked: "What will happen to the bits of wax if we heat one end of the rod?" Most children up to the age of 12 replied that the wax on the glass rod would melt first (some said that all the bits would melt simultaneously, others say they would melt one by one), because "glass is soft." The wax on the tin tube would melt next because "the heat can pass through inside." The wax on the iron rod would not melt because the heat cannot pass through because "iron is too hard."

Light travels from certain spots (sources of light) toward our eyes. No light comes from objects such as a table, chair, or book. Light also comes from our eyes but it is not the same kind as that which comes from the sun or from an electric lamp. The arrows in Fig. 5.1 and 5.2 were traced by an 11-year-old while explaining how we see and how a mirror reflects. (Cf. adult thoughts about this issue, presented in chapter 1.)

These statements are made by older children whose cultural environment has helped them to construct the concept of light rays. Younger children (7–9 years) do not think of light as something that travels . . . it is everywhere during the day. Consequently, they do not accept graphic representations of light as a straight line. The ray of light has no meaning for them although they all systematically draw the sun with lines radiating from it.

For 8- to 9-year-olds, sound travels from a source directly into our ears without going anywhere else around us (Fig. 5.3).

These types of statements that are commonly termed *spontaneous ideas* are considered by some to be odd curiosities that do not merit much attention, whereas others consider these constructs to be of great importance. Many educators believe that they are obstacles to teaching

FIG. 5.1.   The light goes from our eyes toward the object.

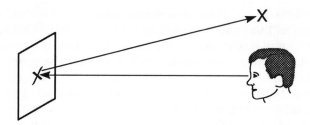

FIG. 5.2.   The light goes from our eyes to the mirror and then toward the object.

FIG. 5.3.   Sound comes directly into our ears.

that must be eradicated like weeds so that the "good grain" can grow. Science teaching educationists in several countries refer to these spontaneous representations in developing teaching strategies.

We are among those who believe that spontaneous representations are important and must be taken into account in teaching science. We do not, however, consider them as weeds. We therefore devote the last part of this section to them.

The Spontaneous Ideas of Children

The ideas of children of the same age and background are surprisingly similar. Although they are personal constructs, they are often taken as collective truths that children do not easily abandon. Even in cases where children appear to accept the adult's explanation it does not last long and they soon return to their own models.

Psychologists, particularly those whose field of study is the development of thinking, take great interest in children's representations. They focus their investigation on them not only because spontaneous representations are considered to be authentic productions of child thought but also because they are resistant to modifications suggested from outside. Yet they do evolve: The representations of a 5-year-old are not those of a 7-year-old. What are the factors that influence a child to change its representations and what are the underlying mechanisms of change?

The answers of the Geneva school to these questions are well known: It is the process of "equilibration." This process that plays a pivotal role in Piagetian theory explains the formation of knowledge and cognitive development in general. In the process of construction, new and qualitatively different levels of equilibrium are attained and these become more and more stable. Each new level is preceded by a phase of disequilibrium that prepares the ground for awareness of conflict or contradiction.

In the 1970s, several studies on the role of conflict in modifying children's representations were done by Genevan researchers (Inhelder, Sinclair, & Bovet, 1974; Piaget, 1974). The predominant hypothesis at this time may be stated as follows: Thought tends toward greater and greater equilibrium and hence cannot accept contradiction that is experienced as a state of disequilibrium. According to this hypothesis, when children find themselves in situations that contradict their expectations or opinions, they initiate processes that will get rid of the contradictions. When these processes succeed in overcoming the conflicts or contradictions, they result in modifications of previously elaborated representations.

The hypothesis on the role of conflict in cognitive development is still considered valid but must be placed in perspective. A situation is perceived as conflictual only if the child's reading of it allows him or her to see it as such. Besides, once a situation is perceived as conflictual one can overcome the conflict in several ways. Although the child may be brought to question his or her views, it does not necessarily mean that he or she abandons his or her ideas and theories . . . a reaction similar to that of scientists throughout history. Here is a particularly pertinent example of this: It is well known that most children up to about the age of 7 assert that light objects float whereas heavy ones sink. Some years ago the following experiment was conducted with a group of children between the ages of 4 and 7 (Papert-Christofides, 1974). After having separated the objects presented into two groups—light objects and heavy objects—and having stated that the light ones would float whereas the heavy ones would sink, the children saw that two objects that had been classified as light sank when put in water. The oldest (6- to 7-year-olds) found this perturbing and deduced that it was wrong to say that all light things float; the youngest (4- to 5-year-olds) remained indifferent to the phenomenon and did not change their opinion; the 5- to 6-year-olds preferred to modify their previous classification—the objects that were judged light but that did not float were, in fact, heavy. In belying the myth that "all light objects float," what could be more convincing than to see objects considered light sink. Yet when confronted with this "evidence" the youngest remained unperturbed, whereas the middle group—those that we consider the most enlightened in this example— overcame the conflict simply by changing the classification of the objects concerned: Because they sink they are heavy . . . coherence and equilibrium re-established! One is certainly not going to change one's opinion about the laws of nature just because of this!

With the development of science teaching in the 1960s, educators became interested in the spontaneous representations of children. As science teaching is introduced earlier and earlier in school, the importance and weight of the child's spontaneous representations is felt more and more. These are often considered to be obstacles in the transmission of knowledge required by the curriculum. Hence, one of the main questions that teachers are faced with is how to cope with the representations of their pupils.

Those faced with this problem usually take one of three different stands:

- The first is one of uneasiness leading to resignation. Because children express their thoughts in a confused manner, teachers have great difficulty identifying their representations from what they say. It is, therefore, not possible to take these into account while teaching.
- The second is diametrically opposed to the first. It is one shared by several teachers in France who do not seem ill at ease with the way their pupils express themselves. For them, the child's representations are the point of departure in teaching.
- The third position has neither the pessimism of the first or the enthusiasm of the second. It may be summarized thus: The teacher should help children to express their representations clearly and then take these into consideration while teaching. However, one needs to know much more about how these representations form and evolve in order to make the best use of them.

Having said this, we examine more closely the second attitude, not only because it is becoming widespread in France, but particularly because it reflects the relationship that exists between representations and teaching, between spontaneous knowledge and school knowledge. We take the liberty of borrowing a few quotations from Sanner (1983) that describe the existing situation well:

> Hence the representations of children should be taken into consideration.
>   On the grounds that identifying their representations is too compli-
> cated, that it implies individualised teaching which is quasi-impossible
> with the large number of pupils per class, one could knowingly choose to

make a clean sweep of approximate representations and replace them by solid, new knowledge that is unrelated to these approximations.

This is the choice made by certain traditional methods of education. The other point of view is that the child's representations form the first link that he can establish with the knowledge that we seek to make him acquire. In the end, it is this representation, this personal model that must develop and that we cannot ignore, for the simple reason that by ignoring the representation we do not get rid of it; it is simply repressed. (pp. 17–18)

Sanner also said:

"We mentioned the term 'initial representations.' What does it mean? It is time to set aside certain misunderstandings.

This question is all the more important because the teacher acts as the mediator between the learner and knowledge. He is mainly concerned with what he wants to teach the child, with what the child should know and not with what he already knows or thinks he knows and which is really the starting point.

In order to make use of these representations in teaching, one needs to know the "initial state of the child," the child's conceptions prior to the teacher's intervention so as to provide supports for them while determining the teaching strategy. (pp. 17–18)

The aim is clearly stated: it is to make the child's representations evolve by creating situations that are conflictual for the child.

Bringing the child's representations to light does not serve any purpose unless one is able to make them evolve.

In this educational perspective, the problem is to start with conflicts that the child really feels, either individually or when confronted with peers. (Sanner, 1983, p. 18)

Psychologists and educators seem to agree that counter examples, contradictions, situations that give rise to cognitive conflict play an important role in the development and modification of children's spontaneous representations. Their differences lie mainly in the identification of the representations themselves . . . psychologists consider them to be authentic constructs of child thought and hence precious objects of deep investigation; educationists consider them to be obstacles in the way of teachers. They wish to know them in order to fight them better, to eradicate them, and to replace them with true knowledge. We discuss this position further to show that it is an aberration.

Take children who have not constructed any spontaneous representations concerning the physical phenomena to which they are exposed daily. This would mean that they have not reflected on their experiences and have not constructed any knowledge. What educator would dare to think that he or she can easily teach such children what he or she considers valid?

Now take children who have spontaneously constructed correct representations. They would be geniuses capable of inventing by themselves the science of their time and perhaps that of the future, too. For such individuals, teaching would not serve any purpose.

Fortunately, our pupils are individuals who construct their knowledge normally and naturally without waiting for permission to do so. To consider these products of reflection an obstacle to teaching seems unreasonable to us.

As for the position that seeks to make the child's representations evolve through cognitive conflict, it reflects an atomistic conception of knowledge. If this was right, one could replace one unit of knowledge with another without much difficulty. It would be sufficient to confront the child with evidence that contradicts that unit. However, the structure of knowledge seems to be organized in a way that does not allow unit by unit modifications. An "observation" that contradicts a belief or opinion is an object of assimilation rather than a source of modification. When situations give rise to convictions, subjects consider their formulation of them as truths and they take their place in an organized cognitive framework. Any new suggestions coming from observed facts or from other people are accepted only if they can be integrated into cognitive frameworks that give them credibility.

All teaching, particularly that of the experimental sciences, encounters numerous obstacles. The most serious ones come from the fact that even those teachers who are aware of the psychological phenomenon of "assimilation" in the Piagetian sense and who accept it as a fundamental mechanism in the construction of knowledge, do not take into account the fact that what they teach will certainly be assimilated (i.e., deformed in various ways by each pupil).

To this day, there is no method of teaching we know of that is structured around the representations that pupils elaborate on the basis of what is taught. The only information that teachers have about these representations is their feeble reflection in examination papers.

DESCRIPTION OF OUR WORK
AND THE MAIN RESULTS OBTAINED

At the end of high school, I was illiterate in most fields especially in scientific ones. Yet I was considered a good student. What a waste of time spending one's childhood and adolescence on a school bench for so little. Later on, as a psychologist I worked with normal children who yet failed at school and had thus become very insecure and unhappy.

I believed naïvely that it was possible to change teaching methods and attitudes in the classroom by talking to teachers. It took me some time to realize that such discussions were usually no more than monologues in front of people either too polite or too indifferent to contradict. Most teachers have no clear ideas about what, how, and why they do what they do. Their work is weighed down by traditions.

At this time I was also working with Jean Piaget at the Center for Genetic Epistemology. The first research I contributed to was on the development of logical structures that led me to doing a doctoral dissertation on children's ability to argue and to demonstrate the validity of their assertions.

Later on, the theme of study at the center was causality. For 4 years, a team of 20 mathematicians, physicists, biologists, logicians, and psychologists collected data and discussed at length the role of the object in the construction of knowledge. Each member of the team focused on the aspect that he or she considered important: Piaget wished to study the operations that the child attributed to the object, the physicists studied the child's natural thought and spontaneous representations, whereas the logicians tried to apprehend the underlying logic, and so on.

In 1972 it was decided to introduce experimental science teaching in Genevan primary schools. It was to be part of an integrated course called "Environmental Studies," which included elements of history, geography, and biology. Prof. Michael Hubermann, then head of the Education Department of the University of Geneva, asked me to collaborate with the primary school team working on this project. It was in this context that I was able to do the work described here.

The aim of the team was to develop a primary school curriculum for experimental sciences on the basis of Piaget's description of the child's conception of physical reality . . . a curriculum that would respect the cognitive development of children and their reasoning capacities at different ages and operational levels.

I tried my best to explain that one could not transpose directly to curriculum development, a theory that was not developed for educational ends and whose data was collected in a context very different from that of a classroom. It was difficult proving my good faith in taking such a stance. The negotiation that followed was long and tumultuous. Finally, it was agreed that for a period of 1 or 2 years (prolonged to 4 ½) I would be allowed to experiment in the primary school classes of the canton of Geneva in collaboration with the teachers.

For me, this work was a contribution to the reflection of all those who seek to render school less repressive, to reduce the stress it puts on children, and to allow children to learn with understanding.

Like a good pupil of Piaget I thought it was important to let myself be guided by children. Hence, I created situations in which I could observe and talk with them. They were also situations that facilitated the construction of physical knowledge and onto which one could graft science teaching.

My main aim was to observe children's activity when it is provoked by material put at their disposal, by recall of out-of-school experiences and by nondirective discussions in the classroom. In this way I hoped to understand the kind of problems that children come up with and the manner in which they try to solve them.

Observing Provoked Activities

There were three phases to our work in the classroom:

- Observation of unguided activities of the children;
- Discussion of certain notions and problems related to these activities;
- Suggestions of tasks.

I describe these three phases and make some comments on the method used.

Observation of Unguided Activities

During three to four weekly sessions of 45 minutes each, the children of one class worked individually or in groups doing what they chose to with the materials supplied by the experimenter. The material was made up of a variety of objects that did not in themselves impose any particular form of activity on the children. On the contrary, the children could attribute diverse meanings to the objects and combine them in numerous ways.

We worked mainly with four types of material.

- In the first year, it was material related to the theme of "water." There were large plastic troughs filled with water and a multitude of objects: stones, pieces of wood, string, bits of styrofoam, nails, pins, modeling clay, cottonwool, paper, transparent tubes of different lengths and diameters, funnels, plastic yogurt cups, straws, aluminium cake moulds.

- In the second year, the main theme was "weight." Besides common objects like pieces of wood of various shapes and sizes (rods, cubes, planks), curtain rods, styrofoam, cork, string, scissors, nails, hammers, glue, paper, cardboard, thumb tacks, rubber bands, and marbles, there were also pulleys, balances, and spring scales.
- The main theme of the third year was "mixing and mixtures": there were different kinds of liquids (water, oil, vinegar, methylated spirit), different powders (flour, sugar, salt, sodium bicarbonate, dyes) and different grains or seeds (lentils, wheat . . .). In addition there were newspaper, wax paper, rags, cottonwool, pipettes, straws, plastic spoons, immersion coils for heating water.
- In the fourth year, the main theme was "motion": The material was made up of wooden planks (250cm × 40cm), blocks, balls of various sizes and weights, and cones. This material was supplemented by objects that the children brought in themselves from one session to the next. Apart from the scales, pulleys, pipettes and water heaters, all the objects could be put to a variety of uses and this is what in fact occurred.

These sessions were called "free or spontaneous activity sessions" not only because the material did not limit the form of activity but also because the expectations of the adults concerned (i.e., the experimenters and teachers) were not circumscribed: Any activity undertaken by the child was accepted as being potentially interesting. This premise resulted in a neutral and well-disposed attitude to whatever the children did. The children quickly sensed that unlike what often happens in the usual lesson, there wasn't one "right answer" known to the adult that the child had to guess. The aim of this lesson was simply to do something of interest and to follow through an idea as far as possible. This was indeed the "right answer" expected by the adult, but it allowed each one to go off in the direction that he or she considered right and interesting for him or herself and not for another person.

The term *free* should not be taken to mean that there were no constraints. The fact that the children worked in the presence of two or three adults, that they were in school—a place loaded with meaning— was in itself a constraint, although, in this case, they could work on the floor, in the classroom or outside in the corridor, or on the stairs. The instructions given at the beginning of the first session of free activity also specified certain limits: "You are free to do as you like, but take care not to destroy the material because the others need to use it after you. Try to do things that seem interesting to you."

Discussion of Activities

During the unguided activity sessions the children were confronted with a variety of problems related to several concepts. These problems were often subject to some concrete activity such as trying to build a tower as high as possible using bits of wood of various shapes and sizes with a base that is much narrower than the first floor of the tower. Or, trying to make objects float that normally sink.

Sometimes they came across a problem unexpectedly. An example of this was when several children put seeds into a cup containing a little water, which they left in the corner of the classroom to see what would happen. Would the seeds sprout and, if so, in how many days? On the third day, they found, to their great surprise, that there wasn't any water left. They then wanted to know where it had gone.

Thus, concepts of equilibrium, buoyancy, evaporation, and many other concepts were present in a jumbled way in the children's activities without being explicitly introduced. During the free activity sessions we contented ourselves with making a note of these problems and we took them up later one by one in discussions with the whole class. These were called "synthesis sessions."

After three or four free activity sessions, when the children seemed to have exhausted the possibilities of the material and did not know what else to do, we would suggest that the whole class should come together to discuss some of the problems we had observed while they worked and that had seemed interesting or difficult to solve. We would then describe the observed problem situations. The children who had experienced them filled in the details. The others gave their opinions on how one could tackle the problem better, study it, and maybe solve it. Some of these suggestions were viable experimental plans. Examples of these discussions are given later.

Suggestions of Tasks

These synthesis sessions inevitably led to proposals for further activities. However, not all the children wished to do them. Therefore, we compiled a list of some of the more elaborate activities undertaken by the children during the free activity sessions and proposed these to the class. The children could choose from among these or from the ones proposed during the synthesis sessions, or they could invent others. These sessions were called "proposed activity sessions."

A few remarks about the method used and the population of children we worked with. The *method* is one of "observation of provoked behavior" largely inspired from the classical method called "clinical observation and interviewing" developed by Piaget and his collaborators. Essentially, it consists of making children talk. During the free activity sessions we went from one group to another with a tape recorder and asked "What are you doing?" We tried to ensure that all the members of the group said something. We only said things like "I haven't understood properly. Can you explain that to me better?" or "Tell me a little more about this." Sometimes, in order to get another child in the group to talk, we would say, "Perhaps you can help your classmate. You tell me what he wants to say." Each group of children was interviewed in this way two or three times during each session. Very often the children called out to us without awaiting their turn in order to share their findings or a problem with us. Whenever they asked the question "Why . . . ?" we refrained from giving them any information and even less an explanation. We would simply say "What do you think?" or "Your classmate over there has the same problem. Go and talk to him about it." We realized that when children asked "Why?" they always had their own answer to the question and were only too pleased to express it.

The utterances of the children were transcribed and analyzed. They served as the central thread of the research that helped us to understand to some extent what they did and thought.

Piaget's clinical method was developed for individual interviews and we had to adapt it to working with groups. In doing this we were careful to preserve the spirit of the method; that is, not to suggest things to the child and to maintain the same positive attitude to all responses whether they were correct or not, asking the child to explain his or her own thoughts as precisely as possible.

The population with which we worked were the children of Genevan primary schools which comprise five grade levels: Grades II, III, IV, V, and VI (Grade I is part of kindergarten). The age range was from 7 to 12–13 years. Every year each set of materials was tested with children in all five grades. No children participated twice. There were 20 to 25 children per class. Each class participated in at least three spontaneous activity sessions, one synthesis session and one session of proposed activities.

The Spontaneous Activities

All the children we observed were very active during the free activity sessions. In order to bring out the meaning of their activities we divided them into categories according to the aspect of the activity that seemed to capture the child's attention. Besides the problem of simplification inherent in any classification process, we were confronted with the problem of having to break up a continuous process into smaller units of activity. Another important difficulty arises from the fact that the mechanisms and the course of the mental activity underlying what is observable, escape awareness almost entirely even for the subject who performs the activity. Our analysis had to be based only on observations and on the verbal remarks and explanations that the children provided.

We propose to distinguish three aspects in an activity: A, that which comes from the child performing the activity (actions, establishing relationships, operations, etc.); O, that upon which the activity is performed, usually called the object; ; R, the result or the outcome of the interaction between the subject and the object.

When the activities concerned are not logicomathematical but concrete or physical as in the case of almost all the activities undertaken by the children in the context in which they were placed, the result is partly due to the specific characteristics of the object and partly due to the actions of the subject. The following diagram summarizes this:

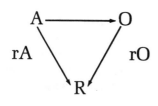

Where A is the activity of the child:
      O is that upon which the activity is performed
      R is the outcome
      rA is the part of R that derives from A
      rO is that part of R that derives from O

While engaged in an activity the child seems to take more interest in one of these aspects than in the others. For instance, his attention is directed toward the result he wishes to obtain and he does not take into account sufficiently the steps to take or the objects to be used. Or, his attention is focused on his own actions and the result is apparently of secondary importance. Obviously, the other aspects are not absent from his cognitive field; they seem to occupy a peripheral position as though they were not relevant to that particular situation. On the basis of what appeared to be the focus of the child's interest during a given activity, we have established eight types of activities.

Types of Activities

The following is a list of types of activities.

1. Activities focused on A. The child busies himself pouring water from one container to the other, mixing liquids, heating, gluing, nailing things together, and so on. He concentrates on what he is doing and seems quite content. When one asks him "What are you doing?" he often replies "Nothing" or "I don't know," but goes on with the activity quite seriously.

This type of activity may be termed *play* or *assimilating activity* in the Piagetian sense. The child exercises previously constructed schemes on the material. One gets to know objects by acting upon them. In other words, one attributes meaning to them by assimilating them into ones existing schemes.

If a concrete product comes out of this activity the child usually gives it a name and asks to take it home. For example, the child is caught in an activity of gluing or nailing things together, and then decides that the outcome is a "tower," a "machine," or a "camera." It is only as an afterthought that he names his construction, which often does not even vaguely resemble the real thing . . . somewhat like the scribbles of a 3- to 4-year-old that are afterwards said to be a boat, a house, or a mother.

2. Activities focused on R. The child is bent upon obtaining a particular result and all his actions are done with this aim in mind. For example, he is intent on transferring water from one container to another with the help of a straw or a plastic tube. The way he goes about doing it seems to be of little importance to him although this will to a large extent determine his success. This is why, if he succeeds once, he is unable to repeat what he did. When he tries to explain what happened he imagines actions that are incompatible with the result obtained.

Various types of constructions fall into this category. The child decides that he wants to make a crane, a slope, a scale, a tower, and so forth. He goes about its construction using the objects and means at hand. He is not concerned with the particular nature of the objects or with the method of putting them together. The result usually resembles the model in shape but is rarely functional. Sometimes the child starts by imitating just the shape of the model and then goes on to modify his construction so that it is able to move like the model.

3. Activities focused on O. This type of activity may be termed

exploratory. The child tries to understand how something works and chooses to explore objects found in the material provided—balances and scales—or objects constructed by him—the siphon, for example.

4. Activities focused on r. The child attempts to establish a relationship between the product and the process or the sequence of actions performed. When asked to explain what he is doing, he often replies "I want to see what happens." When asked if he has an idea of what might happen he often says he has one but that isn't clear. We could call these "experiments to see what happens."

For example, the child puts different sorts of seeds into a cup and adds water. He does the same with another cup but covers it with a piece of cardboard. Although he usually refuses to make predictions he expects certain things to happen and in the previous example he is surprised when at the next session he finds that the water has diminished and the seeds have increased in volume.

5. Activities focused on rA and R. The child tries to obtain a given result by varying his actions. For example, he throws the seeds forcefully into one container of water and lowers them gently into another. He explains that he wants the seeds to float and he assumes that the way he puts them into the water plays a part. Another example of this was seen with several Grade IV children who were surprised to find that oil floats on water. They tried to invert the layers by pouring oil first and then carefully adding water in the hope that thus the oil would stay below the water.

6. Activities focused on rO and R. In an effort to determine the role of the object in obtaining a given result, the child tries to reach the same result by varying the objects used. For example, seeing that froth forms when vinegar and sodium bicarbonate are mixed together, he tries to mix in other powders like flour, sugar, or salt and to replace the sodium bicarbonate with one of them. He also tries a substitute for vinegar by mixing sodium bicarbonate with methylated spirit.

7. Activities focused on rA, rO, and R. The child tries to reproduce a result that either he or a fellow classmate has already obtained. He knows which objects to use and which rules to follow due to earlier observations and manipulations. One could call these activities *consolidating activities.* For example, the child obtains froth several times in a row by mixing vinegar and sodium bicarbonate, or he obtains three very distinct layers by putting water, oil, and finally alcohol into a goblet.

This last category is qualitatively different from the preceding ones. The course of action is chosen on the basis of an assertion that the child believes to be true and that he would like to prove to himself and others.

The sequence of activities takes the form of clear logical steps in an experimental plan.

As we can easily see, these eight types of activities may be regrouped into three broader categories: (a) Activities that focus on the action of the subject, on the object or on the result (i.e., Types 1, 2, and 3); (b) activities through which the child seeks to single out the factors that have contributed to a particular result; which steps contributed to it and the role the objects played in it (i.e., Types 4, 5, 6, and 7); and (c) activities that are experimental (i.e., Type 8).

Frequency and Evolution of Spontaneous Activities

Activities belonging to Categories a and b just listed were found with children of all grades. During the free activity sessions only children of Grades V and VI undertook activities of the third category. However, during the synthesis sessions even Grade II children undertook such activities.

Some Grade II children indulged only in Type 1 activities and some of Grades V and VI undertook Type 8 activities. However, the large majority performed all types of activities. In general, activities belonging to Categories a and b were more frequent with the younger ones, whereas Categories b and c were more frequent with the older ones.

The second session of free activity saw an increase of Category b and c activities for all groups of children. This is not surprising because the first session was most appropriate for Type 1 activities. During the third session of free activity a number of children seemed to have exhausted their interest in the material and did not undertake new activities: They contented themselves with observing their classmates.

As far as the sequence of types of activities within one session is concerned, one observes all possible combinations. Some start with Category b and c type activities and end with Category a. Others do just the opposite. Some undertake Category a activities at the beginning and end of the session and Category b and c types in between or vice versa. It is noteworthy that the majority of children start with activities belonging to Category a and go on to Categories b and c.

Before going any further, we illustrate the eight types of activities described earlier with a few examples. We mentioned earlier the difficulty in demarcating "activities" within the continuous process of individual or group work. This is why in the following examples an activity of one type is often prolonged into an activity of a different type. During the free activity sessions, the children mainly explored the material provided and although this exploration went through different phases it was uninterupted.

Pa., Grade II

This was the first session with material concerning weight. One of the first activities that Pa. indulged in was putting nails into a cork. He fixed three nails into a cork and said "It's a flashlight" (Type 1).

Comments. It is clear that Pa. is interested in the action of pushing nails into a cork. Cork is resistant although it is not hard. The name given to the result of this activity seems of secondary importance. In all probability, Pa. did not intend to make a flashlight and his construction did not resemble one.

However, Pa. probably drew some information about the objects used in this type of play. Fixing nails in wood, cardboard, styrofoam, or cork is not quite the same thing. The difference and the difficulties one experiences are due to the objects upon which one acts and not the action itself.

Ma., Grade II

This was the second session with material concerning water. Ma. puts several objects into the water and blows through a straw. She points out that the objects that float move. This activity is very common among children of all levels when working with this material (Type 1).

Ma. then sucks water into a straw, puts a finger underneath and tries to pour the water into a cup that is floating in the trough by turning the straw over while keeping her finger on the top. To her surprise the water does not fall out. She shakes the straw but the water flows out only when she removes her finger. All excited, she narrates, "I sucked water into the straw and then I put my finger on the end and the water didn't fall out. When I don't put my finger, the water falls" (Type 2 and 3).

Another girl, attracted by Ma.'s recent discovery, joins her and together they fill a cup using straws (Type 7).

A boy from the same group starts transfering water from one container to another by the same method but instead of a straw he uses a thin plastic tube (by chance?). He is delighted with his success and soon abandons the idea of transfering the water. Instead he struts around the class displaying his tube full of water, open end downwards (Type 6).

Comments. Ma. probably intended to use the straw as a container for transporting water. In fact, she wanted to construct something. However, the particular attributes of the straw cause her initial project to fail and put Ma. before a physical phenomenon that she and her classmates find interesting. This prompts several members of the group to take up various activities linked to the understanding of this phenomenon.

St., Grade II

These were the first and second sessions with material concerning water. For several minutes St. keeps blowing into the water through a thin tube (Type 1).

While attempting to transfer water from one container to another using the tubes provided, one child tells how his father drew petrol from his car with the help of a tube. To the surprise and admiration of his classmates he succeeds in making the siphon. Several children, including St. try to do the same. St.'s initial occupation of blowing into the water is transformed into another activity with a specific aim: to transfer water from one container to another with the help of a plastic tube. This is how she goes about it: She puts one container filled with water and an empty one on the table. She dips one end of the tube into each container. She then takes the end of the full container, blows into it and quickly puts it back in the water. This is how she describes what she wanted to do and why she failed: "I took the end out and blew into it. Then I put it back. The water should have flowed through. All the water should have entered the tube and then climbed up it. But it didn't want to climb . . ." (Type 2).

At the second session, St. busies herself with filling a tube with the help of a funnel and blowing into it. From what she says we gather that it is not the act of blowing that is now of interest to her. Her statements are related to what one may call the "behavior" of the water in the tube: "I blow in here and the water comes out there." She wants to draw a diagram and adds arrows to show how the water flows. She draws them wrong and explains "I made a mistake. It's in the other direction" (Type 3).

Afterwards, she modifies her activity by putting a ping pong ball into the funnel. The water comes out, making the ball go up and down (Types 2 and 3).

Comments. St.'s activity during these two sessions is coherent. Her attention was drawn to her classmate's activity of constructing a siphon and she tries to imitate him. She does not succeed and attributes her failure to the water's behavior ("It did not want to climb"). It is this problem that St. wants to understand. So, during the second session all her activity centers around how water "behaves" in the tube.

It is worth noting that our attempt to help St. make a siphon (we did not want to leave her with having failed), was not essential for her. She wanted to understand, not just to succeed!

M.-P., Grade III

These were the first and second sessions with material concerning weight. M.-P. "plays" with the two-pan balance for a long time, putting various objects into the pans and comparing their respective weights (Type 3).

Then she decides that she wants to construct a balance. She takes two wooden bars and a small plank to serve as the base. She has difficulty nailing the pieces together and one of the adults present helps her a bit. The result is a T that can stand upright and of which the horizontal bar is not very mobile since it is nailed to the vertical bar. M.-P., pleased with this result (Type 2) takes two containers and attaches one on each end of the horizontal bar. She takes a few metal disks and starts weighing (Type 3). She then comes over to us and says: "I put four disks in one container and five in the other and they weigh the same." We suggest that she put the same number on each side. She takes one out of the container in which she had put five. The balance remains immobile. We press to make it tilt a little to the left, then to the right. The bar maintains the position that one puts it in . . . M.-P. is obviously bothered. "It isn't right" she says. "Is this what the other balance does?" we ask, referring to the one in the material. "No," replies M.-P. and goes off to re-examine the model (Type 2). She comes back and tells us, "The balance doesn't have any nails. It has a special part." Time having run out, she carefully puts her balance away in the cupboard and takes it out again at the next session.

This time M.-P. removes the nail and replaces it with a screw. The bar is now much more mobile (Type 2).

Comments. Children from Grades III through VI often construct such balances; the models differ from child to child. Most of them first try to reproduce the external appearance of the balance without taking into account how it works. Only later on do they tackle problems of mobility and sensitivity.

We noticed that not one of the children thought of using the many metal disks we supplied as a unit of measure to weigh other objects.

They all confined themselves to comparing the weights of two objects. Even Grade VI children were slightly surprised when a big object turned out to be lighter than a smaller one. However, they had no difficulty attributing this difference to the substance of which the object was made. This semiconflict is not surprising because we know through psychogenetics that it is only toward the age of 11 or 12 that weight becomes dissociated from volume.

C1., Pa., J.-L., Ce., Grade IV

These were the first, second, and third sessions with material concerning "mixtures." These four boys work together in a corner of the room and take great interest in each other's activities. However, each one has his own containers and makes his own mixtures (Type 1).

J.-L. is less enterprising than the other three and works under Ce. Gradually, the other three get interested in three different phenomena:

- the formation of froth,
- the formation of layers, and
- the speed at which grains sink in different liquids.

We describe here the activities of each of them during the three sessions of free activity.

Ce. is busy mixing different things together (Type 1) and suddenly exclaims, "Look, madam, it makes froth." From then on he tries to determine which element is the cause of this phenomenon and pays attention to what he puts into the mixture (Type 6).

During the second session, Ce. and J.-L. try to reproduce the froth. They know that vinegar and sodium bicarbonate together are responsible for this. They prepare different mixtures and add vinegar and sodium bicarbonate thus obtaining froth of different colors and viscosities (Type 6).

Then they switch to making "lines" (i.e., layers). With the help of a pipette they put different things into containers and succeed in obtaining "inverted layers" (i.e., the bottom layer in one container is the second layer in the other). Their explanations refer to the notion of weight (Type 4, 5, and 6).

At the third session, Ce. is absent and J.-L. either watches the others or undertakes Type 1 activities.

C1. explains what he is doing thus: "I put oil and green dye in the cup. The oil is on top though I put it in first." The experimenter gathers that C1. is surprised and asks "The oil is on top and you put it in first . . . you find this strange?'' C1. explains: ''But it must be lighter than the dye''.

Then C1. imitates Ce. in making froth (Type 7), but remains interested in the formation of layers. He tries to form different layers by varying the content of the mixture (Type 6). During the second session, he talks of the layers he was able to form by mixing green dye with salt (Type 6).

At the third session he tells us: ''I mixed oil and brown dye and I put in some salt which stayed at the top.'' He expresses his surprise: ''Normally, salt is heavier and should sink, but it stayed on top; why, I don't know'' (Types 5 and 6).

Pa. observes that grains put into the liquid in one cup sink faster than those he puts into another. He repeats this several times saying, ''There, it sinks faster. Here it sinks slower'' (Type 7).

Then he adds other things to the liquids in the cups, thus modifying the consistency of the mixture and puts the grains in again (Type 6). At one point he exclaims: ''Oh, that's super, it goes down faster.'' He continues for some time and explains: ''I'm trying to see if they go down slowly or quickly.''

Pa. starts the second session by making layers and then stirring them up to get rid of them (Type 4). He tells us: ''The colors (layers) go back to their places. I mixed them up to see.'' Afterwards he tries to make froth like Ce. using a cup in which he had already formed layers: ''I wanted to do the same as Ce. but with several layers, and not the same ones.'' He says you need flour, green dye, brown dye and sodium bicarbonate. He adds: ''The bicarbonate makes the froth with the vinegar and the dye'' (Type 6).

Later he goes back to making layers (Type 7) but this time instead of stirring to efface them, he tries to invert them by pouring the contents of the container into another to see if the top layer stays at the bottom (Type 4). Because the layers remain the same he tries pouring more quickly (Type 4).

During the third session, Pa. makes dough (Type 1). While playing, he talks about the density of the dough and the ingredients that modify it: Flour makes it more dense, salt does not change it, and liquid makes it less hard (Type 6).

Later on in the session he takes a cup and puts several things into it, making statements that show that the problem of the formation of layers still intrigues him: ''I don't understand at all. When you look from here (the side) you'd think it (barley grain) is on top and when you look from here (the top) you would say it is underneath'' (Type 3).

Comments. If we consider the evolution of the activities of this group, we see that they start with Type 1 activities at the beginning of the first session and devote most of the second and third sessions to activities of Types 4, 5, 6, and 7.

Pa. offers a good example of undifferentiation between that which is due to the activity of the subject and that which is caused by the specific nature of the object. Such undifferentiation is a normal phase in the construction of cognitive objects.

Ils. and Is., Grade V

These were the first, second, and third sessions with material concerning mixtures. Ils. and Is. work together at a desk that is slightly sloping. Using one pipette filled with vinegar and another filled with colored water, they let some drops fall onto waxed paper and watch what happens: The drops slide together and fuse into one (Type 3). The two girls assume that it is the "stronger" liquid that attracts the other: "First they were separate and we saw that the drops of vinegar came together more easily than the drops of paint. Then we mixed the two and we saw that the vinegar was stronger. So we're going to put more vinegar."

Afterwards they make the hypothesis that the inclination of the paper can play a role and that it is not just the "strength" of the liquids concerned that determines their mutual attraction. "Perhaps, it also depends on the position of the paper." They move to a horizontal table and start varying the amounts of liquid (Type 6). This lasts about 35 minutes. Then they try to see if drops of oil, vinegar, and colored water stay on the surface of a piece of cottonwool or are absorbed by it. They also vary the amount of liquid (Type 3). Toward the end of the hour, inspired by what they had observed while watching their mothers cooking, they do the following experiment: They put different types of grain into a cup of cold water, saying "We saw that when mother makes soup she puts some barley into it and the grains swell. So we want to see if the same thing happens in cold water. We've also put in wheat and oats" (Type 8). Because they know the effect will not be immediate, they keep the cup aside and look at it a few days later.

At the next session Il and Is. tell us "We looked at the grains on Monday and there was already no water left. We're going to add some more water now to see if it evaporates or if it is the grains that absorb it. So we're going to cover the cup" (Type 8).

They spend the rest of the session doing another experiment: They take three cups and put sugar in one, sodium bicarbonate in the second, and flour in the third. They add water in each and make observations about the changes that come about. Then they add some vinegar in each. This produces froth in the cup with sodium bicarbonate. Once the froth disappears they make remarks about the level of the liquid (Type 6). Then Il. says: "I've got an idea; we could see if it's the powder that does it or the vinegar; let's put just water and vinegar together." They do this and nothing happens. Then they add bicarbonate of soda and conclude "It's the powder that makes the bubbles, this is proof, it's the powder" (Type 8).

At the third session they voice their observations of the grains they had soaked in a covered cup. They consider the level of water to be a relevant indicator of whether the water evaporated or if it was absorbed by the grains and turn their attention to this. "We looked on Saturday [a school day in Geneva] and it (level of water) hadn't changed. This morning we looked again and it was still the same." From this they infer: "Last time the water had evaporated" (Type 8). We asked them if they thought that the fact that the water level remained unchanged showed that the grains did not absorb water. Is. replies: "If they did, it's normal that the level goes down. It's like us when we drink, we take it into our mouths and the level goes down."

They then mix together sugar, salt, sodium bicarbonate, flour, dyes and vinegar and the mixture froths (Type 5). Next, they add oil and say: "It doesn't change anything. It doesn't want to mix with the rest" (Type 6). They stir the contents to mix the oil, but do not succeed (Type 4). "It stays on top of the rest, it doesn't want to have anything to do with the other things. Perhaps it doesn't mix because it's greasy. I remember, we put colored water on wax paper and saw that certain things came together. Perhaps that was also because it was greasy, since oil that is greasy doesn't mix with other things."

Comments.   This example is typical of Grade V and VI pupils who derive hypotheses from their activities that they then try to verify with experiments. These are simple but, in general, methodologically sound: Knowing that grains swell in hot water, they put them in cold water, to see what happens in different conditions of temperature. Some days later the grains had swollen, but an unexpected result captured the children's attention: There was no more water in the cup. What happened? Did it evaporate? Was it absorbed by the grains? Because the cup was uncovered the first time, they cover the cup the second time assuming that they have thus neutralized the evaporation factor. The conclusions drawn from this experiment are incorrect not because of a defective method but because their knowledge about volume is insufficient.

A1. Grade IV

These were the first, second, and third sessions with material concerning weight. A1. declares "I want to construct a huge 8, a train that runs on rails, turns and comes back." He uses cubes to support the curtain railings that serve as rails and constructs two slopes along which a marble can roll (Type 2). The two rails form a 100° angle (see Fig. 5.4). The bend caused a few technical problems because the slope had to be gentle enough for the marble not to bounce off the lower rail when falling onto it. However, A1.'s main problem had yet to be solved: how to get the marble to come back to the starting point and set off on its path again. A1. spent the second half of the first session and the whole of the second grappling with this problem but did not succeed. He used means that appeared quite farfetched: strings attached to the top of the blackboard, springs, and the like. The partner who started working with him soon gave up and A1. spent a lot of time contemplating his construction alone.

During the third session, three others join A1. in constructing a very long circuit. They say: "We want to make a circuit that starts here, that goes there and then continues. This bar will go in the other direction and there (in the middle of the third bar) we'll make a sort of jump (springboard) so that the marble bounces up and falls back on the same bar." They had to modify their construction as many as four times due to technical problems. In fact, they considered a certain length necessary to give the marble enough impetus to jump. In order to obtain the required length, the starting point had to be high enough and this created problems of instability (Type 2).

Comments. A1.'s construction attempts reveal his spontaneous representations concerning inertia and energy conservation. His wishes and expectations encountered resistance from the objects and this set him thinking, particularly during the second session. Although the project he had for the third session was much more modest, it probably reflects the same concern he had from the start: how to make

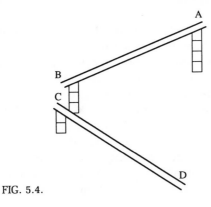

FIG. 5.4.

the marble climb back up through its own impetus by constructing a springboard.

Da. Grade VI

There were the first, second, and third sessions with material concerning weight. Da. wants to make a crane. He chooses the material he thinks he requires for this and works by himself. His first product resembles a crane in appearance (Type 2) but Da. is not satisfied because he would like it to work like a crane as well. He gradually refines his construction until, in the third session, he is able to make a crane with a system of ropes and pulleys that lifts and lets down a basket that can hold objects. It also has an arm that rotates from left to right within an arc of about 200°.

Comments. Da., A1., M.-P., and several other children were absorbed in construction tasks that demand accomodation to a model that the children perceive as more and more complex thus creating a growing number of specific problems. The tasks are of the type proposed in "problem-solving" situations except that in the latter case it is the adult who proposes the problem whereas in the tasks we describe it is child himself who gradually makes his goal more and more complex. The children seek an optimal level of difficulty based on the awareness of how certain mecanisms function (Da., M.-P.) and also on certain principles of physics (A1.)

Even if Da.'s knowledge of the working of a crane was not enhanced by his construction activity, it was not in vain for he learned many other things. In any case he needed a lot of imagination to find solutions to practical problems with the modest means at his disposal.

The Role of the Adults

As we mentioned earlier, the two or three adults present during the free activity sessions took notes on what the children did and tape recorded the children's explanations about what they were doing and what they wanted to achieve. To make them clarify their explanations we simply said "I don't quite understand—can you explain that to me better?".

In the preliminary phase of our work, we asked children to write or illustrate what they had done at the end of each free activity session or at least to put down what they had found interesting. The children did this unwillingly. Their drawings were poor and did not convey anything of importance. We soon gave up asking them to do this, much to the dismay of the teachers for whom the written word has unquestionable value. *Scripta manent* is true, but it is because they do not have wings!

But how different the verbal explanations were. Children are eager to talk and will sometimes interrupt others who are not quick enough. The recordings reveal their excitement, their enthusiasm, their hesitations, and the birth of new ideas. We also captured moments when a child's effort to explain underlying ideas brings him or her to realize things and causes him or her to take another direction, the first one suddenly appearing to be a dead end: "Ah! But no . . . I've got another idea" . . . and the child would cut short his or her explanations and go off to the table where the material was kept to pick up other objects and start other activities. Sometimes he or she would only talk about it at the next session, when he or she thought his or her activity was advanced enough to deserve communication.

The children found that talking to someone about what they were doing was quite natural and this type of adult intervention integrated well with their activities. Talking requires the translation of thoughts and intentions that may be global and visual into a linear form; it also means defining things that are vague. Besides, the form of presentation must be acceptable to the person to whom it is addressed and convey meaning to him or her. Thus, the fact of having to explain stimulated the children's activities. This type of adult intervention together with the synthesis sessions, is, in our opinion, most enriching.

The Synthesis Sessions

The children's spontaneous activities served as a starting point for discussion with the whole class. These discussions were meant to bring the children to focus on certain themes and problems encountered earlier and to open the way toward other related questions. All the spontaneous activities do not lend themselves to this; activities belonging to Categories b and c were found most suitable.

Our choice was guided by the frequency of the activity, the possibility of investigating it with the modest means at our disposal, and through experiments that the children could plan and execute independently. The aim of these discussions was also to place children in a situation of socialization of knowledge. They can discuss their difficulites, express opinions, and listen to those of others; they can defend and confront points of view according to certain rules of logic of which they must become aware. New experiments can be proposed and then discussed again by the whole class, and so on. These discussions, which require a certain mastery of group dynamics on the part of the adult leading the discussion, aim to encourage the children to formulate questions clearly and to be critical regarding assertions. This happens quite naturally because for every point the children will make different statements.

We must not lose sight of the fact that a given term such as *weight, force, evaporation, pressure,* and the like, can carry a more or less vague meaning for the child using it. Vague and also different, not only from the adult's meaning but also from that of other children.

The various notions have, for each child, their own history. They evolve and are related or fused with one another in strange ways. Each child's notions have their particularities but we can make out a development common to groups of children according to their age.

The children's discussions—contrary to the idea of so many adults that children are unable to discuss—were always very animated, spontaneous, and enthusiastic. Children talk with great force and sincerity, and they handle counter-example arguments readily. In their every day life the less-gifted children have learned to remain quiet: The teacher has a tendency to favor correct answers and to immediately sanction incorrect ones. This is certainly not conducive to discussion among pupils. We therefore welcome with equal good will all the children's responses and propositions. Our intervention is limited to requesting further explanation and to asking whether everyone agrees with what is being said. Very often the outcome of discussion is a proposal for a new experiment to see who is right. (Because of differences in developmental level, the class usually divides into two groups upholding different opinions.)

Thus, experiments were designed by the whole class and entrusted to one or two groups of children to be done. The merits of these synthesis sessions lay in the elaboration of experiments.

The following is an example of such discussion with the youngest group of Grade II children:

During the discussion the following question is raised: "Does a grain of rice have weight?". Two answers are given simultaneously: "yes" and "no." We ask what could be done to find out who is right. One girl suggests an experiment: "Take a glass of water and put a grain of rice in and see what happens. If it sinks, it has weight. If it floats, it doesn't." Everyone accepts this suggestion enthusiastically. After a few seconds a boy objects to this procedure saying, "We won't be able to see anything that way. Ships certainly have weight, but they float!". Everyone is impressed by this argument and start talking among themselves. Then a little girl takes the floor and the others stop talking to listen to a new suggestion: "We'll drop the grain of rice on the floor.

It it makes a noise, it has weight." We ask if the others find that this is a good idea. The boy who had objected to the previous suggestion introduces "methodological nuances": "We must choose what we make the grain fall on. If it falls on cloth no one will hear anything. In any case, we will have to be very, very quiet to hear it."

A week later a grain of rice and an empty yogurt cup was brought to the class. In the midst of pin-drop silence the girl who had made the suggestion stood up and dropped the grain into the cup. Everyone heard the little noise . . . produced by the weight of the grain. The class was delighted and they all agreed that the grain had weight. At this point, another girl comes up to us and says, "I knew it without doing the experiment . . . In a kilo of rice there are many, many grains. They have weight. If several grains together have weight, then one grain alone also has weight. Otherwise, it wouldn't work."

The following is another extract from the transcription of a discussion with the whole class.

During the free activity sessions, three Grade III girls put various vegetables in water to see if they float. A carrot sinks. Co. tries to bring it back to the surface by poking a straw into it and blowing air in. Pa. pokes several straws into a large carrot that is floating at a slant, large end up. She wants to make it float horizontally. Meanwhile, the third girl, Fa., places a potato on a small wooden plank to make it float. Then she puts a stone on the plank to make it sink. We chose these activities to start a discussion on buoyancy with the whole class.

Experimenter	*Children*
Co. do you remember what you did?	I poked a straw through a carrot.
Why did you do that?	To see if the carrot would come up. I blew into the straw and since I'd made a hole in the carrot . . .
And did it come up?	[after some hesitation] Yes, it did. [Pa. interrupts Co.] I had a big carrot that was half afloat. I stuck several straws into it but it didn't come up.
	Co.: My carrot was small and I put three straws in.

But why did you poke straws in?

I'd like to know why certain things float and others don't. Anyone have an idea?

[another child] The straws make it float. They are like buoys on a boat.

Yes . . . but what do the straws do?

Co.: The carrot floats because it has three straws.

Because there is more air? Can you explain that better? Is there more air?

[another child] Because there is more air.

Can you explain what you mean?

The child who had spoken of buoys: I think the straws make things float. It makes the carrot lighter and that makes it float.

If you poke straws into a carrot it becomes lighter?

Yes.

It loses a little weight?

No! But it stays on the water. [another child] One end of the carrot is thinner than the other. So the other end pulls it under. If you put straws on the end it might make it the same on both ends.

What do the rest of you think? Is it a good idea?

[Several children] "Yes" [another child] The other end is thicker. So it's going to go down. Fa. : The thick end was upward. [the previous child] If the other end does the same thing with the straws, it's even heavier. It could make the two ends the same.

On what end should the straws be put? I didn't understand very well.

On the thin end. [the child that had spoken of buoys]: Maybe if we put the straw on the heavy end, it would balance better.

But I don't understand anymore. Where do you poke the straws? Where it's thickest or where it's thinnest?

[Several replies at the same time] Where it's thick!—Where it is thin!

Who thinks one must put the straws where it's thick?

[Seven children put up their hands]

And who thinks one must put them where it's thin?

[Eight children put up their hands]

You're almost at equality. What must we do to see who is right?

We have to try.

The Proposed Activities

There are at least three reasons why these proposed activities are not a return to guided instruction. The activities are chosen among the ones that arose spontaneously. The way that they are formulated leaves children free to go about them as they wish. If the children prefer to do something else they can do so.

From among the spontaneous activities occurring in a given age group, we chose those that seem to us to be the most interesting and then presented them in written form to all the children of the same age group. Here are some examples:

- make a spring scale,
- make a "building" as high as possible starting from a base made of only one block. The block has to be exactly in the middle (the following drawing is given):

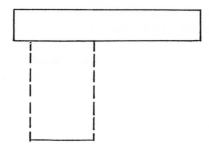

- choose one of your books and find out how much it weighs.
  Afterwards weigh two books together, then three books, then
  four, and finally five books together.

The first two examples are activities we proposed to Grade V and VI
children the third activity to Grade III children. We chose the scale-
making task because the children that had had the idea showed some
very interesting difficulties in constructing a graduated meter-stick.

The weighing task was considered interesting for 8- and 9-year-olds
(Grade III pupils in the canton of Geneva) because this is the age at
which most children have constructed invariance of "weight" that is
not yet understood as a force. Moreover, quantification and measurement are still relatively undeveloped. We noticed that at this age most
children make only qualitative weight comparisons when weighing
two objects on a pair of scales. Several children using a letter scale
found that three books weighed 500 (Kilos for some children!). They
were not at all surprised to find that four books also weighed 500 and
that five books weighed no more. The synthesis session that followed
turned out to be very interesting.

The following question immediately comes to mind: Why not start
straight off with the proposed activities? Why not just use the spontaneous activity sessions as a field for observation and to make a list of
activities for each grade level, and then propose these to the pupils?
The idea is tempting and much more acceptable and adapted to today's
schools. We did in fact try this sort of procedure: We gave the same
tasks and problems to children that had never been engaged in the
spontaneous activity sessions. Of course we provided them with the
same material as the experimental groups. The results were very
significant. The work of the control group children—those who had
not experienced the free activities—was very similar to the work that

children of the same age showed during the first session of free activities. The children in the experimental groups on the other hand, took up the tasks we proposed with both seriousness and joy. Several of them even invented analogous tasks. It thus appears that for children at primary school level, interacting with objects is a deep intellectual and emotional need, and that the proposed activities are most meaningful when they follow the free activities.

Introducing Restrictions

One reaction of teachers was to question the need for such a wide variety of objects put at the children's disposal and the need to allow such a variety of activities. They seemed ill at ease with the nondirectivity of our approach. They preferred to reduce the number and types of objects included in the material and to give more specific instructions. For example, they proposed having troughs of water with a few bottles available one day and at the next session replace the bottles with plastic tubes and so on.

We interpreted this reaction as an implicit request for introducing restrictions. We tested two types of limiting interventions:

1. To give instructions at different points in time during the free activity sessions, and
2. To reduce the variety of material provided.

The first type was tested with two groups of Grade III and VI students while working with the material concerning mixtures. Before the children came in for the first session we wrote on the blackboard, "You must not use all the substances simultaneously. You are allowed a maximum of three at a time." When the children came in we told them what we usually told a new group: that they could look at all that there was on the table and do whatever they wanted with it. This time we added, pointing to the blackboard "Don't mix everything at the same time. Take two or three things. You can do lots but with a few substances at a time."

The reaction of the Grade III group was straightforward: They listened quietly to what we had to say and as soon as we had finished they rushed to the table with the material and completely ignored the restriction we had imposed although it was still up on the blackboard. They acted exactly like other Grade III children to whom we had not said anything about the number of substances they could take at a time.

The Grade VI children expressed their discontent by saying, "What can we do with just three things?'' Some tried all sorts of tricks to bypass the restriction. For instance, they would make a first mixture and say, ''That counts as one,'' thus being able to use as many substances as they liked. Others stopped short and did nothing on their own—they just watched other children.

The same instructions were given to two other Grade II and VI groups, but this time it was at the beginning of the third session of free activity. The instructions were respected on the whole. The activities undertaken were less varied than those of other groups during the third session, but of a fairly advanced level in general.

The second type of restriction was tried with Grade II and III groups while working on the material concerning weight. We had observed that children below the age of 9 found hammers, glue, and nails irresistible. Most of their activities consisted of nailing and sticking— a useful bit of information for parents and craft teachers! We took away these attractive objects and found that Grade II and III groups that did not have these available at the beginning developed other, more elaborate activities.

A hybrid form of directivity was tested with Grade II experimental and control groups. We asked the experimental group to solve a particular problem and we also reduced the variety of material available; the other group had the same material as before. Both these groups had experienced two free activity sessions without any restrictions. We found that the experimental group worked better.

Because the experimental groups often required two or three normal free activity sessions before introducing restrictions, there was a considerable amount of work involved and we could not replicate and vary the types and timing of the restrictions as much as we would have liked to. Nevertheless, these tests clearly show that nondirected activities are not a waste of time because children who have had the opportunity to experience them can later work in a much more structured manner. This comes to light particularly during the third phase of proposed activity. Besides, the attempts to channel activities from the start (restrictions at the very first session) seem to go against their nature because the younger ones do not take these into account at all and the older ones who try to respect them are hampered.

In conclusion, we believe that the child's margin of liberty is increased by providing a large variety of objects that can be put to different uses. However, we do not hesitate to remove objects that impose what may be called *mono-activities* (like nails and glue for the younger ones) or to add others if we think that they will have a positive influence by allowing children to intensify or to further develop their activities.

AND THE TEACHERS

We carried out our experiments in schools of the canton of Geneva where teachers are not encouraged to innovate. A so-called "good" teacher is one who goes through the curriculum at a reasonable pace and is able to complete it by the end of the year. As with other countries there are obviously teachers who are more independent and who make maximum use of the liberty that the system allows. On the other hand, there are those who take shelter behind a structure that is quite rigid and follow the prescriptions of the method and the inspector step by step.

Our way of working was, to say the least, unusual and in spite of all our discussions and explanations, it remained incomprehensible especially as far as its aims are concerned. As a matter of fact, our concerns, the problems we tried to investigate, the information we wanted to gather, and so forth, were meaningful within the theoretical framework that was ours but that did not coincide with that of the teachers. Seeing the enthusiasm of the children, the teachers were reassured that something positive was happening, although they could not specify what. This prompted the teachers to cooperate with us even though they could not attribute a positive meaning to most of what was happening in their classrooms. Yet they were not lacking in good will or intelligence.

There are three aspects of our work that were the least acceptable to teachers:

- the role of the adult;
- the diversity and divergence of the children's activities; and
- the insignificance of the immediate, observable result of the activity.

The role of the teacher is a key role. This is not specific to Geneva: The teacher knows, talks, dictates, organizes, judges. Even in classes where children work in small groups the role of the teacher is usually not drastically modified. The teacher's place at the center is reinforced by his or her educational theory (Fox, 1983) if the teacher believes that the learner is an empty vessel to be filled, an amorphous bit of clay to be suitably molded, or an "outsider" to be initiated in a strange land by a good guide.

The adult, and more so the teacher, always tends to intervene, to correct, to guide, to explain, in one word, to "teach" when he or she thinks that the other, particularly if it is a pupil, could do better. This is one of the main functions of the school: to transmit to new generations in a minimum amount of time that which humanity has taken centuries, milleniums to construct. Criticizing this would be absurd. However, it is regrettable that the transmission of knowledge practiced by schools continues to be inspired by empiricist theories of learning, in spite of psychogenetic evidence that challenges the very foundations of these theories.

In an empricist, associationist, and/or behaviorist perspective, the errors, failures, or difficulties of pupils are viewed either as their own responsibilities or as shortcomings of the method of instruction. In a constructivist psychogenetic conception, on the other hand, there are different kinds of errors and difficulties, and teachers' tasks are to differentiate those that they have to correct and those that they have to respect because they result either from children's levels of development or from the progress teachers are making in the organization of children's knowledge.

Although neither the method nor the content of teaching can be directly drawn from genetic psychology, rethinking these in the light of it opens new vistas of unsuspected value. Educators resist adopting them, however, because they lead to positions that go counter to traditional schools. Let us consider the teaching of experimental sciences that concerns us here. In introducing this in elementary school we must take into account the following psychogenetic datum: Up to the age of about 14–15 years, the cognitive structure of the child is in the course of construction and is therefore different from that of the adult. Due to this difference, it is inevitable that everything the teacher tries to transmit is deformed.

Even if the role of the teacher is amenable to variations, it remains the key role in the class. It is not surprising, therefore, that the peripheral role we had throughout the free activity sessions was somewhat shocking to teachers. They wanted to guide more. They wanted to reply to questions by giving the information that the pupil asked for, but that is impossible for several reasons. They would have preferred to "select" the activities they considered "scientific" and interesting. They would have liked the children to produce drawings and written texts. They wanted to build a curriculum. They also thought that the children must be frustrated—although there was nothing in their behavior that indicated this—because the outcome of their activities was not final and definitive; not even a stencil to sum up what had happened in class! Yet the children's attitude during their work was one of enthusiastic involvement. They were so absorbed with what they were doing that they completely ignored the adults present, thus proving their autonomy. This was disconcerting to teachers who were convinced of the necessity of guiding their pupils sometimes to an extent that would bother anyone who was not completely resigned to submission as a comfortable stance.

The children's attitude during our research was just the opposite of the frustration that teachers feared, such that even the most skeptical among them admitted that something essential was taking place in the children's minds. One of them confided that he feared that the children would do nothing worthwhile and that they would waste their time. Afterward he added that with the training he had received, he did not feel capable of keeping track of such a variety of projects and even less of answering their questions. But quite obviously the children did not express the need for the teacher to keep track of their projects and rarely asked them questions. Pseudo-answers like "And what do you think?" seemed to satisfy them amply and they would give us their opinion smilingly . . . they certainly had one and it counted more than ours.

We think that the obligation to reply to pupils' questions that teachers impose on themselves together with the fear of not being able to finish the course in time is the basis of their directive attitude. Children must go "this way" because that is the way the teacher knows and in which the teacher feels secure and at ease. Any other way might lead to a dead end. In these conditions how can we expect children to develop autonomy, critical understanding, and creativity?

Throughout our experiments and especially during the free activity sessions, children experienced *cognitive liberty,* which was for most of them a new experience in the school setting. To choose a goal and to try to attain it in ways that seem adequate, to set one's own subgoals, to explore, to stop, to fumble, to reconsider, to start again . . . and all this at a pace that is not imposed by someone else. Such a process requires that the learner coordinates, establishes relationships and inferences, in a word, it implies intense cognitive activity. To make plans for attaining a goal that one has chosen according to one's own interests and cognitive capacity is an emotionally enriching experience very different from the frustration of following the written instructions of an exercise, especially because one does not often understand the logic behind the series of manipulations that, like magic, give the result predicted by the teacher. The projects elaborated by the children according to their representations of physical phenomena using their own intellectual tools were almost never understandable at first glance to the adult observer. For instance, two Grade IV boys spent 2 hours constructing a weighing device that was so unusual that an adult could not recognize it without the explanation of the boys. There was a chair on top of a table, a string attached to the top of the blackboard at one end and to the leg of the chair at the other, a pulley that could slide various objects along the string and a stopper against which the objects butted. All this was connected to an indicator that moved along a ruler . . . the more centimeters it indicated, the heavier the object because it fell with greater force. Both of them tried repeatedly to perfect the device. It was only toward the end that they began to question the relationship they believed to exist between centimeters and grams. It took us some time to understand what they were getting at but their joy and enthusiasm revealed the interest it held for them. Would it be absurd to think that most of the time the classroom situation is just the reverse of this? Doesn't the adult propose activities that make sense to him but not to the children?

Our discourse on the importance of proceeding independently with a project that is undefined at the start and that may remain undefined for some time was new to the teachers and seemed topsy-turvy to them—like the fact that we did not pay attention to the outcome of the activity but stressed the underlying process of reflection. To allow children to direct their activities themselves, to permit them to explore, to try out things, and on top of this, to attribute to the process a certain formative value for the their intelligence and knowledge, was considered nonsensical, almost a desecration of the school!

And what about evaluation? What were we going to test? But why must we evaluate? Another scandal: How can one conceive of educational practice without evaluation? Yet all the teachers agreed that evaluation was sometimes absurd because one did not assess what one thought one did and wanted to do. They agreed that it served mainly to reassure the parents that teachers were in control of what happened to the children, to reassure teachers that they could judge what their pupils had learned and all this at the expense of the children. For to feel judged constantly makes one insecure, causes stress, teaches one to adopt bad intellectual habits. It is better to learn by rote than to understand, it is better to pretend that one has understood, it is better to cheat than to fail a test, and so on.

Free activities leave teachers perplexed. On the other hand, the synthesis sessions impressed them. How is it that the children could discuss, even those of Grade II? We explained that this was no mystery: One simply had to discuss children's problems and not adults' problems. In addition, one had to accept false statements as willingly as those that seemed correct to us.

As for the proposed activities, they were accepted half heartedly: Yes, but, not all of them seemed "scientific" to the teachers.

In conclusion, if the teachers reacted in the way they did, this was because they assimilated what they saw in their classrooms to their empiricist theoretical framework. According to the empiricist view, the only way to teach is by *giving* well-organized information. This assumption is widespread all over the world, and very few educators even question its validity.

However, children's behavior in and out of the classroom suggest to observant teachers what Piaget has called *construction*, the idea that knowledge is built by the child from the inside rather than being absorbed from what the teacher says, what is written in books, or what is contained in objects.

We believe the Piagetian constructivist view is more in harmony with the child's natural process of learning. Our hope is therefore that schools change their approach to teaching in a fundamental way. For this change to occur, an essential step will be a change in the way educators think about the teaching-learning process.

The implication of this statement for teacher education is complex and far reaching. I do not go into the details of teacher education, as this topic is discussed in depth in other chapters of this volume. Suffice it to say that teacher education cannot be undertaken by mere transmission of constructivist theory. The mechanisms of learning are the same for children and adults. Teachers, too, must construct their own knowledge of teaching and learning from the inside.

Some Thoughts on Teacher Training

My experience in this field is based on ("voluntary") in-service training workshops organized during school holidays where I met teachers actively searching solutions to the problems they encountered in their classrooms. It was at that time that I came to understand the ideas teachers have about the teaching–learning process. Even though these conceptions may not be stated explicitly, they are nevertheless apparent in not only teaching practices but also in the way teachers discuss their work.

The most general and widespread of these ideas is that teaching consists of *giving*. The one who learns—the pupil—is seen as someone who *accepts*—more or less willingly—that which is offered to him or her by the teacher.

This conception, as old as school itself, was consolidated by the empiricist philosophy of Hume and Locke and by Anglo-Saxon behaviorism. However, there are many ways of giving: elegantly or clumsily, in massive doses or little bits at a time, according to a specific order, or randomly. One can present the content more or less agreeably, one can propose it or impose it. The one on the receiving end can accept the content with enthusiasm or unwillingly, with hidden or overt hostility.

Didactic methods are concerned with this giving–receiving transaction: Unfortunately, however, this market is not controlled by the laws of supply and demand.

A much less widespread idea is the one inspired by Jean Piaget's theory of knowledge, and which equates learning with construction: The learner constructs his or her own knowledge. Thus, the pupil chooses from what is given to him or her whatever is useful and adequate for the construction of a particular notion. This conception gives rise to two tendencies. One, more radical, considers the teacher and his or her knowledge as a particularly valuable and important "object" in the pupil's environment. The pupil can interact with this object in the same way as he or she does with books and other didactic materials that may be found in the classroom. In his or her interaction with pupils, the teacher does not play a secondary role; on the contrary, the teacher has to show originality, imagination, and creativity in transforming the classroom into a rich and stimulating microworld. It is the teacher and his or her knowledge who keeps this microworld alive and functioning.

The second tendency that is less radical and more acceptable within traditional schooling is one in which the role of teacher is that of a guide who invites his or her pupils to follow him or her to a land unknown to them but full of wonders. Pupils build their own knowledge, but follow the teacher's direction.

Alongside their ideas about the teaching–learning process, teachers have specific and more or less elaborate conceptions about the methods that are appropriate for particular subject matters. For instance, there are four different ways in which experimental sciences can be taught:

1. The first way is in an essentially encyclopedic manner. For example, the solar system is composed of nine planets revolving around the sun. The sun is a star . . . the difference between a star and a planet is pointed out. Our earth is a planet and it has a satellite called the moon, and so on.

2. The second way is through illustration, which is very often combined with encyclopedic information: A model of the solar system is presented and used to explain the movements of the planets.

If the lesson concerns an object in our immediate environment, the pendulum for instance, the encylopedic method would consist of a description: "Imagine we have a string at the end of which we attach a metal ball." The teacher then describes its movement and the factors that modify the oscillations. The illustrative method simply substitutes the "imagine" with "look" and "watch." The teacher's explanations are accompanied by the manipulation of a device.

3. A third way of teaching is centered around carrying out guided experiments. The more complex or costly experiments are demonstrated by the teacher in front of the class; others are done by the pupils themselves, individually or in groups.

Thus, taking once more the solar system as an example, after a brief introduction the teacher presents some classic experiments on gravity, the moon's phases, lunar eclipses, and so forth.

As to the example of the pendulum, the pupils can do their own experiments to determine the factors that influence the rate of oscillation. Afterward the students and the teacher try to formulate their observations and the experimental results.

These three different ways of teaching science are not incompatible and are often used by the same teacher.

Depending on the topic or the time of year (whether or not exams are near) the teacher will give preference to one or the other of these methods.

4. A fourth approach, more recently developed and not yet frequently used, is derived from the idea that the purpose of science teachers is to introduce children not only to scientific knowledge but also to the ways through which it is constructed. Thus, teaching science also means providing children, even the young ones, with opportunities to get a taste of what research is all about. The pupils set up problems, make hypotheses, and carry out experiments, look for information, take part in discussion.

In other words, the children continue in the classroom the intellectual goal that they have pursued since their births, that is, understanding the world around them.

The experiment we described in the main part of this chapter illustrates this teaching approach.

The demand on the teacher is much greater in this last manner of teaching than in the previous ones. It is not easy to transform a classroom into a laboratory where 20 pupils or more can do interesting work.

When thinking about these approaches to science teaching we must take into consideration the obstacles specific to each one.

The first two are very vulnerable to a general obstacle that is the distortion of what the teacher is trying to transmit. Any given information, any demonstration of guided experiments will be interpreted, extrapolated, and modified by each child in his or her own way. This distortion is due to the process of assimilation.

Another obstacle, particularly relevant to the third type of teaching, arises from the fact that most of the planned and guided experiments do not correspond to the pupil's own interests or questions, nor to his or her own ways of investigating them. The experimentation that goes on is more like following recipes than true experimental activity.

In the fourth way of teaching, the main obstacle is the great diversity of activities undertaken by the different groups of children. This diversity is quite natural considering the numerous paths an individual can follow in constructing knowledge. However, it can make teachers feel very insecure unless they have been trained specifically for this kind of teaching. Furthermore, in certain countries, this diversity may be considered intolerable because it makes it difficult to follow a curriculum and to evaluate the pupils' progress.

There are both affinities and incompatibilities among the different conceptions of the teaching–learning process and the four ways of teaching science.

Obviously, if teachers consider that their work consists essentially of giving or handing out knowledge, they will prefer an encyclopoedic way of teaching.

On the other hand, if teachers see themselves as guides, they will prefer the third teaching approach. The lessons will be organized around guided experimentation and results will be formulated with the help of the teachers.

Is it necessary to add that only the fourth way of teaching is compatible with the constructivist conception of the learning process in which the teacher acts neither as a dispenser of knowledge nor as a "guide" on a journey of knowledge, but as an interlocutor who encourages children to construct their own knowledge. Before specifying the requirements of teacher training, it is necessary to decide for what form of teaching the teachers are to be prepared.

REFERENCES

Fox, D. (1983). Personal theory of teaching. *Studies in Higher Education, 8*(2), 151–163.

Inhelder, B., Sinclair, H., & Bovet, M. (1974). *Learning and the development of cognition* (S. Wedgewood, Trans.). Cambridge, MA. Harvard University Press

Papert-Christofides, A. (1972). *La preuve: étude expérimentale sur la psychogenèse de l'argumentation demonstrative* [Proof: An experimental study on the psychogenesis of demonstrative arguementation]. Geneva: Médecine et Hygiene.

Piaget, J. (1926). *La représentation du monde chez l'enfant* [The child's conception of the world]. Paris: PUF.

Piaget, J. (1974). *Recherches sur la contradiction* [Experiments in contradiction]. Paris: PUF.

Sanner, M. (1983). *Du concept au fantasme* [From concept to phantasm]. Paris: PUF.

Author Index

187

Subject Index